MW01258134

They're Not Even Close:

The Democratic vs. Republican Economic Records, 1910-2010

Republicans Harm America's Economy — It's Now a Proven Fact!

Eric Zuesse

Hyacinth Editions

Published by Hyacinth Editions
NYC 10022
hyacintheditions@mail.com

ISBN-13: 978-1-880026-09-0
ISBN-10: 1-880026-09-0
e-book ISBN: 978-1-62111-724-7

CONTENTS

4:   Democrats Are Better for the Stock Markets

10:   Democrats Are Plain Better for the Economy

20:   The Grand Old Prejudice Causes Economic Stagnation

41:   Democrats Reduce, Republicans Increase, Government Deficits

47:   Republicans Actually Win by Punishing the Nation

106: Conservatism Is Based Only on Faith

115: Trickle-Down vs. Percolate-Up Economics

123: Republicans Harm More than *Just* the Economy

124: Would Romney Be Better than Obama?

126: References/Sources

What the Economic Record Shows About Republican and Democratic Economic Policies, from 1910 to 2010

America's two major political Parties, Democratic and Republican, are highly competitive with each other when it comes to winning political office; but, when it comes to these two Parties' respective records of economic performance, there is no competition at all – they are virtually opposites of each other, regarding their records on unemployment, the average length of a person's unemployment, investors' gains-losses in the stock markets, and other major economic variables.

Democrats Are Better for the Stock Markets

Ever since Fred C. Allvine and Daniel E. O'Neill published their "Stock Market Returns and the Presidential Election Cycle" in the September 1980 *Financial Analysts Journal,* financial analysts have noted that there has long been a remarkable correlation between Democratic Presidents and booming stock markets, vs. Republican Presidents and poor stock markets.

This will be a book about data, and so it is going to be filled with references to sources such as that article. These references are necessary because Republicans will naturally resist *believing* data that show their economic beliefs to be *false*. Republicans resist believing the overwhelming data that global warming is happening, and so their beliefs about ecology are false; they will *similarly* resist the overwhelming data, presented here, showing that Republicans in political power harm the nation's economy. So, it is important for Republicans to have *as easy access to these data as possible*, in order to minimize their misery encountering the falseness of their own beliefs. We are therefore obliged to *cite* these sources, to make it as easy as possible for them to know that, unfortunately, their economic beliefs *are* false – unequivocally and undoubtedly false, as shown by the economic record. Furthermore, Democrats will *also* need to check these data, in order to test (and in their case, confirm) that their economic beliefs are *true*. So, this book is filled with data you can check.

The most exhaustive academic study to probe the question of how well the U.S. stock markets perform under Democratic and Republican presidents was the 1 June 2000 "Political Cycles and the Stock Market," by Pedro Santa-Clara and Rossen Valkanov, available at several places on the internet, which was subsequently published by the *Journal of Finance*, October 2003. This study employed two broad stock market indexes from the University of Chicago Center for Research in Security Prices (CRSP). The "value-weighted" index emphasizes the prices of large-corporate stocks; the "equal-weighted" index doesn't distinguish between large and small corporations, and is therefore a better indicator of how well investments in medium and small-sized U.S. corporations perform over time. As the original version of the paper phrased its basic finding: "Using data since 1927, we find that the average excess return of the value-weighted CRSP index over the 3-month Treasury bill rate has been about 2 percent under Republican and 11 percent under Democratic presidents — a striking difference of 9 percent!

This difference is economically and statistically significant, does not seem to be due to small-sample estimation biases, and is robust in subsamples. The results are even more impressive for the equal-weighted portfolio, in which case the difference in excess returns between Republicans and Democrats reaches 16 percent." Interestingly, the study found that though investors in large corporations did much better under Democrats than under Republicans, investors in smaller corporations did *spectacularly* better under Democrats. This means that Democrats provide vastly greater economic opportunity for entrepreneurs, and for other businesspeople who have not, as of *yet*, reached the status of being members of oligopolies. This is precisely the kind of economic benefit that the Republican Party has customarily said that they provide and that Democrats don't.

Then, Sean D. Campbell (of the Federal Reserve Board), and Canlin Li (of U. Cal. Riverside), issued their FEDS Working Paper No. 2004-69 in November 2004, "Alternative Estimates of the Presidential Premium," and reported that, "During periods in which annual market volatility has been in excess of 25%, approximately 11% of the time between 1927-1998, Democratic administrations have experienced vastly better stock market performance than Republican ones," and that this difference largely accounted for the superior Democratic stock-market performance over that long period. Factoring out this superior performance during volatile markets, "In the case of large stocks we find that the estimated Democratic return premium falls from 8.93% per year ... to between 2.95% and 5.41% per year, depending on the specific estimator employed. In the case of small stocks the estimated premium falls from 15.67% in the case of OLS [ordinary least squares] to between 4.85% and 12.10% per year." Those differences too are enormous. This study's "Abstract" opened with the following summary of the prior literature on the subject: "Since the early 1980's much research, including the most recent contribution of Santa-Clara and Valkanov (2003), has concluded that there is a stable, robust and significant relationship between Democratic presidential administrations and robust stock returns. Moreover, the difference in returns does not appear to be accompanied by any significant differences in risk across the presidential cycle." Thus, beyond any reasonable doubt, from the economic standpoint, Democrats in the White House are far better than Republicans, notwithstanding the common myth to the contrary, that "Republicans are good for business."*

Also, Carol Vinzant of slate.com, using a different data-set, carried the analysis back a *full century*, to 1900, and came up with *essentially the same finding*, that Democrats are far better for investors than are Republicans, and that this is true not only for presidents, but for congresses; i.e., a Republican congress is bad for investors. Headlining, on 4 October 2002, "The Democratic Dividend: The Stock Market Prefers Democratic Presidents to Republicans," she found that "Democratic presidents have produced a 12.3 percent annual total return on the S&P 500, but Republicans only an 8 percent return. In 2000, the *Stock Trader's Almanac*, which slices and

---

* America's major media, and the intelligentsia press, have assisted the Republican Party in this deception of the public. A good example was James Surowiecki's "The Financial Page" in the *New Yorker*, on 20 November 2006, headlining "Elective Economies," which argued — entirely by mis-citation of sources and data — that whether Democrats or Republicans are in power has actually little if any affect on the performance of the stock market. For example, Surowiecki said: "A study of Presidential elections since 1928, conducted by the finance professors Pedro Santa-Clara and Rosson Valkanov, found no systematic difference in the way the market has reacted to the election of Democratic and Republican candidates. ... It's foolish, then, to expect elections to cure ailing economies or wreck healthy ones." One could hardly imagine a more blatantly false characterization of that study, whose abstract stated, "Contrary to the widespread opinion that 'Republicans are good for business,' we find that the average excess returns in the stock market are higher under Democratic presidents." The researchers stated: "After controlling for a vast number of macroeconomic variables that have been shown to affect returns, our results remain unchanged; the difference between excess returns during Democrats and Republicans is still around 10% for value-weighted returns and 20% for equally-weighted returns, statistically significant, and very stable over different sample periods." They called their findings "striking." This is the study which James Surowiecki said "found no systematic difference in the way the market has reacted to the election of Democratic and Republican candidates" in Presidential elections. No wonder Americans believe things that have been disproven.

dices Wall Street performance figures like baseball stats, came up with nearly the same numbers (13.4 percent versus 8.1 percent) by measuring Dow price appreciation. (Most of the 20th century's bear markets, incidentally, have been Republican bear markets: the Crash of '29, the early '70s oil shock, the '87 correction, and the current stall occurred under GOP presidents.)"

She continued: "According to almanac editor Jeffrey Hirsch, the presidential party figures are among the most significant he's found. If the stock market were random, we'd expect such a result only one-quarter of the time. 'I don't know why people are convinced Republicans are good for the stock market,' Hirsch says."

Then, she added: "Nor does having a Republican Congress help the market. A Democratic Senate showed returns of 10.5 percent (versus 9.4 percent for a GOP upper chamber), and a Democratic House returned 10.9 percent versus 8.1 percent for the Republicans."

Furthermore: "Real GDP growth follows the same pattern. Since 1930 (the first year decent data is available), GDP growth was 5.4 percent for Democratic presidents and 1.6 percent for Republicans."

A month later, Mark Hulbert at cbs.marketwatch.com headlined on 12 November 2002 "Pop Quiz on Politics and the Markets: Which is better, Republicans or Democrats?" and he used inflation-adjusted data from Ned Davis Research, which showed that, "On average during the 28 years since 1901 in which a Republican has been President and Democrats have controlled Congress, the DJIA has produced a 2.2 percent real return (before dividends). On average during the 25.8 years in which the Republican party has controlled both branches of government, in contrast, the Dow … has produced an inflation-adjusted return of just 1.2 percent." No results were shown for periods when Democrats occupied the White House. Ned Davis Research concluded overall that the average annual market return under a Democratic president has been 7.2%, while under a Republican president the average annual return has been only 3.7%.

On 14 October 2008, a former information graphics editor of *Money*, Tommy McCall, presented, as an op-ed in *The New York Times*, a brilliantly clear chart, "Bulls, Bears, Donkeys and Elephants," covering the past 80 years, half of which had Democratic Presidents, and half of which had Republican ones. The verbal summary of it was: "A $10,000 investment" in the S&P "would have grown to $11,733 if invested under Republican presidents only, although that would be $51,211 if we exclude Herbert Hoover's presidency during the Great Depression. Invested under Democratic presidents only, $10,000 would have grown to $300,671." A blogger, Theodore Gray, at Stephen Wolfram's company, was sufficiently disturbed after reading that, so as to headline two days later, "Stock Market Returns by Party," wherein he searched to find whether there would be lag-times after a President's entering office, which would reverse those findings so that Republicans would come out on top – even if just barely. He found that there indeed were. However, his employer, wolfram.com, posted, at its corporate website, their own "Stock Market Returns by Party," and showed there, as was usually done, no lag time, and they additionally extended their chart all the way back 111 years, to 1897. 48 of those years were under Democrats, and 63 were under Republicans. Despite there being 15 additional years to grow the value under Republicans than under Democrats, the $10,000 initial investment rose to only $156,017 under Republican Presidents, as compared to $217,202 under Democratic ones. The site, **http:demonstrations.wolfram.com/StockMarketReturnsByParty/**, also enabled one to tweak the data with whatever underlying assumptions one might happen to prefer, which was what Mr. Gray was doing in his blog-post. One of the problems with doing that, however, is that there is already a lag time between a Presidential candidate's winning the White House, and his actually becoming President. Even on a President's first day on the job, there has already been plenty of time for companies to adjust their plans so as to affect the economy.

On 22 February 2012, Bloomberg News bannered "Stocks Return More With Democrat in White House," and Bob Drummond reported that, from 1960-2012 (till February 21st), $1,000 invested in the S&P throughout all of the 28 years of Republican Presidencies would now be $2,087, but in all 23 years of Democratic Presidencies would now be $10,920 – a 992% gain, vs. the mere 109% gain under Republican Presidents – and this despite the fact that there were actually five more years for the money to grow during Republican Presidencies. "The Democratic edge is so large that the party comes out ahead even without counting Bill Clinton (the Democrat with the biggest S&P gain) and George W. Bush (the Republican with the worst market record)." The Democratic advantage was enormous: "It's not even close."

Democrats Are Plain Better for the Economy

Adding depth to Vinzant's findings about the economic impact of Party control in the U.S. House of Representatives is the following: On 6 June 2004, under the heading, "If You Want to Live Like A Republican, Vote Democratic (part II)," at **http://rtorgerson.blogspot.com/2004_06_01_rtorgerson_archiv e.html**, the professional investment manager Richard Torgerson calculated the annual inflation-adjusted GDP growth in the U.S. for each year from 1950 to 2003, separately under four categories of U.S. political leadership; and these were the historical growth-percentages in each of the four categories:[*]

---

[*]   The Harvard economist Robert Barro, who is much honored by economics scholars, contradicts Torgerson's calculations that show higher GDP growth under Democratic than under Republican Presidents. Barro is a prominent propagandist for the Republican Party, and in his article in the 8 November 2004 *BusinessWeek*, "Debunking the Myths of the Kerry Campaign," his "Myth No. 4" was "that Democrats do better than Republicans at managing the economy." His supposed corrective to that "Myth" was to assert that, "For the entire post-WWII period, average economic results under Democrats have been similar to those under

were the historical growth-percentages in each of the four categories:

Democratic President, Democratic House: 4.5%.
Democratic President, Republican House: 3.9%.
Republican President, Democratic House: 3.0%.
Republican President, Republican House: 2.1%.

On 22 December 2010, Doug Short at businessinsider.com headlined "Politics And GDP: Which Party Is Really Better For The Economy?" He found that, during the period he examined, 1947-2009, GDP rose:

Democratic President: 4.19%.
Democratic Congress: 3.41%.
Republican President: 2.63%.
Republican Congress: 2.98%.

(The readers' comments posted to this report were almost 100% reality-denial, since the readers at businessinsider.com are overwhelmingly conservative, and since conservatives cannot accept information that contradicts their prejudices – this is why conservatives believe what they do. Conservatives are thus virtual cesspools of falsehoods. This is why conservatives routinely ignore all of the information that will be presented here, indicating that the economic superiority of Democratic over Republican policies is no mere statistical fluke: the fact is devastating to the myth that they have been suckered into. Similarly, when I submitted to *National Review* and the *Wall Street Journal* a news article summarizing the data in this book, it was declined, with no comment.)

Republicans," which was a stunningly weak refutation of the "Myth" even if it were true. However, his statement was even more suspect on account of its remarkable vagueness: What measure of "economic results" was he using, and what was the documentation for this claim? So, I e-mailed Dr. Barro to ask him. Two weeks later, I e-mailed the inquiry again, because he had not answered. He never replied.

In October 2002, a series from Dwight Meredith at **http://pla.blogspot.com/2002_10_27_pla_archive.html#838534 63**, under the heading "Just for the Record," dealt with inflation, unemployment, economic growth, fiscal performance, and shrinking the size of government. The data, from the Government Printing Office, covered 40 years, from Kennedy's first budget in FY 1962 to Clinton's last budget in FY 2001, during which time each of the two Parties controlled the White House for exactly half the time, 20 years. In each of these five categories of measures of economic performance, Democrats outperformed Republicans, especially on fiscal performance (as measured by budget surpluses/deficits) and on shrinking government (as measured by the number of federal employees), which are perhaps the two categories with the biggest long-term economic impacts. The more long-term the perspective was, the bigger the superiority of Democrats over Republicans turned out to be.

For example, to document Democrats producing smaller government as measured by the number of federal employees, that site points to "Just for the Record Part II," which provides the federal workforce numbers, and the changes in those numbers, during each of the Presidents from Kennedy through Clinton, and it concludes: "Under the 20 years of Republican administrations the number of non-defense government employees rose by 310,000. Under the 20 years of Democratic administrations, the number of non-defense government employees rose by 59,000. Of the 369,000 employees added between 1962 and 2001, 84% were added under Republican administrations and 16% were added under Democratic administrations." The only Administration that reduced the number of federal employees (by 310,000) was Clinton (largely because of the recommendations of V.P. Gore's study commission on improving government-efficiency). By contrast, the Republican President who increased the federal workforce the least was Reagan, who *added* 3,000 federal employees. With a long-term record like that, how can anyone with half a brain claim that the Republican Party is "the party of small government"? It's pure lying propaganda, which only a fool would believe.

On 5 October 2002, a more sophisticated statistical analysis, covering "the postwar period 1948-2001," appeared from Kevin Drum (later with Mother Jones magazine), at **http://calpundit.blogspot.com/2002_09_29_calpundit_archive .html#82576526**, in which three different lag-times of "3 Yrs," "4 Yrs," and "5 Yrs" were applied in order to give a more accurate picture of the cause and effect of each President's policies. Results were calculated for three measures: "GDP Growth," "Unemployment," and "Inflation." The conclusion was: "No matter what time lag you choose, Democrats post higher GDP growth, lower unemployment, and lower inflation." (See box below.)

[BOX: Kevin Drum's entry, via the Wayback Machine]

DEMOCRATS RUN THE ECONOMY BETTER THAN RE-PUBLICANS....WHY DON'T THEY GET ANY CREDIT FOR IT?....*Slate* ran a story on Friday suggesting that contrary to popular opinion <u>Wall Street likes Democrats more than Republicans:</u>

Democrats, it turns out, are much better for the stock market than Republicans. Slate ran the numbers and found that since 1900, Democratic presidents have produced a 12.3 percent annual total return on the S&P 500, but Republicans only an 8 percent return. In 2000, the Stock Trader's Almanac, which slices and dices Wall Street performance figures like baseball stats, came up with nearly the same numbers (13.4 percent versus 8.1 percent)....

According to almanac editor Jeffrey Hirsch, the presidential party figures are among the most significant he's found. If the stock market were random, we'd expect such a result only one-quarter of the time. "I don't know why people are convinced Republicans are good for the stock market," Hirsch says.

This is actually an old story, and *Slate* doesn't know the half of it: Democratic administrations, it turns out, manage virtually *every facet* of the economy better than Republicans. To demonstrate this, let's take a look at the three most important economic statistics for the postwar period 1948-2001:

- **GDP Growth** (seasonally adjusted in chained 1996 dollars)
- **Unemployment Rate** (BLS annual figures for civilian unemployment)
- **Inflation Rate** (CPI-U Dec-Dec annual change)

We also need to pick a lag time. In the same way that a pitcher is responsible for runners left on base even after he's been replaced, presidents should be responsible for a few years of economic performance after they leave office.

Fine, but *how many* years? Three seems reasonable — which is how W gets off the hook for our current recession — and certainly no more than five, but in the end it turns out that the exact number doesn't really matter: Democrats do better no matter what time lag you choose. Here's the summary data:

	3 Yrs	4 Yrs	5 Yrs
GDP Growth			
Democrats	3.56%	3.78%	3.71%
Republicans	3.35%	3.16%	3.21%
Unemployment			
Democrats	5.06%	5.04%	5.01%
Republicans	6.16%	6.18%	6.21%
Inflation			
Democrats	3.33%	3.07%	3.20%
Republicans	4.36%	4.60%	4.48%

No matter what time lag you choose, Democrats post higher GDP growth, lower unemployment, and lower inflation.

Given this, is it any surprise that Democrats are the real darlings of Wall Street? The free market may talk softly, but it carries a big stick.

[end box]

Yet another type of analysis was published by Arthur Blaustein in the *Los Angeles Times*, on 19 September 2004, in an op-ed titled "Who's Better in the Driver's Seat?" He considered seven independent measures of a President's economic success, and asked, for each measure, which President, since World War II, has scored the highest? There were six Republican Presidents and five Democrats to choose from since WWII, so the odds for each measure were that a Republican would probably score the highest. But, stunningly, *none* of the six Republicans did. Here were the "prize" winners in each of the seven categories: Highest growth in GDP: Truman. Highest growth in jobs: Clinton. Highest growth in personal disposable after-tax income: Johnson. Highest growth in industrial production: Kennedy. Highest growth in hourly wages: Johnson. Lowest misery index (inflation plus unemployment): Truman. Largest reduction in the deficit: Clinton. The six Republican booby-prize-winners, each scoring 0 for 7, were: Eisenhower, Nixon, Ford, Reagan, Bush I, and Bush II. Only Carter shared their prize.

Furthermore, Princeton University's Larry M. Bartels, who has studied, in more detail than any other researcher, the irrationality of Americans' voting overwhelmingly against their own economic self-interests, and tried hard to explain it, documents in his Feb. 2004 historical study, "Partisan Politics and the U.S. Income Distribution," that there has been a strikingly consistent record of Democratic U.S. Presidents producing a thriving U.S. economy that benefits *all* socioeconomic classes, and of Republican U.S. Presidents producing a stagnant or worse U.S. economy, all of whose meager benefits go to *only* the top 20%, and almost all of whose benefits go to only the top 5%. Dr. Bartels points out, in addition, that *even* the top 5% typically do *better*, in *absolute* terms, under Democrats than under Republicans. During Democratic Presidencies, the real income growth-rates for even the wealthiest 5% of the population, the 95th percentile group, were slightly higher than during Republican Presidencies. However, figures weren't shown for the top 1% — perhaps this tiny group actually does benefit from Republican rule. In any case, the Republican Party has historically increased inequality in the United States, and has harmed all income-groups except, perhaps, the top 1%. Some highlights from this study were published on 26 September 2003 in the *Los Angeles Times*, in an op-ed by Bartels titled "GOP Always Falls Down on the Jobs." Of course, the superior jobs-growth under Democrats has been one of the major reasons for the superior growth in GDP under Democrats; the direct Democratic concern to "spread the wealth" has ended up producing a larger total amount of wealth within the nation; more people earning more money creates a bigger GDP; and that's a major reason why the Republicans' "supply-side" or "trickle-down" policies have failed time after time (except, perhaps, for the few people who are hyper-wealthy, who are the only real beneficiaries of Republican policies, if there *are* any real beneficiaries).

This study by Bartels showed that during the period studied, from 1948 onward, "Democratic presidents have produced slightly more income growth for poor families than for rich families, resulting in a modest decrease in overall inequality. Republican presidents have produced a great deal more income growth for rich families than for poor families, resulting in a substantial increase in inequality." Scholars normally think in terms of a trade-off between equality and productivity, but Bartels showed that, to the contrary, Democratic Presidents enhanced both simultaneously.

Moreover, the difference was greatest at the income-
extremities, and, "On average, families in the 95th percentile
of the income distribution [the very rich] have experienced
identical growth under Democratic and Republican
presidents, while those at the 20th percentile [the poor] have
experienced more than four times as much income growth
under Democrats as they have under Republicans."
Democratic Presidents produced higher income-growth for
each of the five income-categories studied, but the highest
benefits accrued at the lower end. Furthermore, Democratic
Presidents produced far higher GDP growth-rates (4.08% vs.
2.86%) and substantially lower unemployment rates (4.84% vs.
6.35%). Inflation-rates were virtually identical under both
Republican and Democratic Presidents.

Berkeley economics professor Brad DeLong, on 23
September 2008, posted "Brad DeLong's Weblog Archive
Page," with charts comparing annual GDP growth-rate, fiscal
surplus/deficit, stock-market performance, employment
growth, unemployment rate, and equality/inequality, from
the Administrations of FDR, through to the current President
Bush. Democratic Presidents far outscored Republican ones,
on each measure.

In October 2008, zfacts.com calculated and charted
"The National Debt as a Percent of Gross Domestic Product,"
extending from 1950 through to 30 September 2008. The debt
overhanging WWII was near 100% of GDP in 1950, and
declined fairly steadily thereafter until shortly after Ronald
Reagan entered the White House in 1981. At that moment, the
ratio Reagan inherited was around 40% of GDP. It then
gradually soared to about 60% of GDP by the time Reagan left
office eight years later, and to nearly 70% when Bill Clinton
inherited the White House from Republican G.H.W. Bush, at
which moment the ratio went virtually flat and was already
starting to head back down by the end of Clinton's first term,
just as Clinton's tax-hike on the super-rich kicked in, after
which this ratio plunged down to below 60% when Bush's son
George W. Bush entered the White House and the ratio turned

around and, within just a few months of G.W.B.'s inauguration, it soared again, back up to 70% by the end of September 2008, when it skyrocketed, right before Bush bailed out Bear Stearns, A.I.G., and then practically all of Wall Street. Then, of course, the $700 billion emergency bailout of financial institutions was approved by Congress, on 3 October 2008, and this skyrocketing ratio just continued skyrocketing. Clearly, whomever Bush's successor would turn out to be, he would be dealing with an economic situation somewhat like Franklin Delano Roosevelt faced in 1932.

And, as was previously noted, it wasn't just federal debt that soared under Reagan. The three charts from Ned Davis Research, "Total Domestic Nonfinancial Debt as a % of GDP," "Total Credit Market Debt as a % of GDP," and "Private Domestic Non-Financial Debt as a % of GDP," all showed personal and commercial debt soaring shortly after Reagan entered the White House and throughout his Presidency, and then shooting up yet again like a rocket during George W. Bush's eight years.

David Stockman, Reagan's budget chief and the prime engineer and champion of Reagan's tax cuts, quit to write his stunning 1986 confessional *The Triumph of Politics: How the Reagan Revolution Failed*, in which he said (p. 395) "The magnitude of the fiscal wreckage and the severity of the economic dangers that resulted are too great. ... The Reagan Revolution was radical, imprudent, and arrogant. ... By the time of the White House debate of early November 1981, it had become overwhelmingly clear that the Reagan Revolution's original political and economic assumptions were wrong by a country mile. We were headed ... toward a fiscal catastrophe."

The political result of this disastrous policy was Reagan's landslide 1984 re-election. By contrast, the political result of Clinton's 1993 upper-bracket tax hike was summarized by Richard Dunham in *BusinessWeek* on 21 March 2005 (p. 47), saying that congressional Democrats' vote for it "cost dozens of his [Clinton's] House supporters their seats in the 1994 midterm elections — a debacle from which

Democrats have never recovered." Why did these good congressmen lose their seats? The upper-bracket taxpayers poured millions into Republican coffers, and millions of faith-filled fools swallowed the authoritarian line of those GOP ads.

Republican President Ronald Reagan was a fiscal disaster to the American people, and George W. Bush continued Reagan's wrecking of the U.S. economy. Certainly, no other Presidents during the post-WWII era were anything like these two Republicans in terms of damaging America's economy. George H.W. Bush was also bad for the U.S. economy, but that's only because he was a Republican, who generally respected Ronald Reagan, and not because he was, like Reagan and Bush's own son, an outright American disaster. The most harmful American Presidents of modern times — Reagan and Bush II — were also economically the most conservative American Presidents of modern times.

The Republican Presidents Eisenhower, Nixon, and Ford, were also failures in terms of their overall economic performance, but they weren't outright disasters who left future generations of Americans poorer and the nation deeply in debt, as the Republicans Reagan and Bush II did.

On 8 May 2012, Bloomberg's Bob Drummond bannered "Private Jobs Increase More With Democrats in White House," and he reported that, during the period January 1961 through April 2012, in which Democrats occupied the Oval Office for 23 years, and Republicans for 28, private-sector job-growth averaged 150,000/month under Democratic Presidents, and 71,000/month under Republicans.

In other words, there is a striking unanimity among the reports, concerning the correlations between the party in power and the nation's economic performance, as measured in a wide variety of disparate ways. The overwhelming conclusion from all of these studies is: Democrats in power greatly aid the U.S. economy; Republicans in power greatly hurt the U.S. economy.

Few empirical conclusions anywhere in the social sciences are as firmly established as this one.

The Grand Old Prejudice Causes Economic Stagnation

Republicans warned, when President Bill Clinton passed through a Democratic Congress in 1993 tax-hikes on the rich; they warned that the U.S. would become less competitive as a result, and that the nation's economy would nose-dive. But instead, the U.S. became economically more competitive, and the economy boomed. Even the stock market boomed. After Clinton's second year in office (1994), the Dow Jones (DJIA) soared, from about 4,000 at the end of 1994, to about 11,000 at the end of 2000, the biggest stock-market boom during the entire post-WWII era. Republicans in Congress fought against regulations which would have kept speculators honest, and so the later portion of this stock boom turned out to be froth, and the tech-bust resulted. Also, the corporate boom meant that little was achieved in restoring the more-nearly equal distribution of wealth in the U.S. which had prevailed prior to Reagan in 1980. So, the soaring stock market wasn't actually particularly good. However, anyone who says that raising taxes on the rich is bad for the stock market is either a fool, or else is outright lying to advance the interests of the rich at the expense of everyone else.

From a scientific standpoint, anyone who believes that conservatism helps rather than hurts an economy believes a soundly demonstrated falsehood — it can be (and unfortunately is) taken *only* on faith; i.e., on prejudice. There is simply no scientific basis on which that widespread public and academic belief holds up.

Steve McGourty, in his "Figure 3" at **www.cedarcomm.com/~STEVELM1/usdebt.htm**, showed "Change in Average Revenue and Spending By Administration, Johnson to Second Bush," and consistently, revenue into the government from taxes was higher, and spending by the government was lower, under the Democrats, Johnson, Carter and Clinton, than under the Republicans, Nixon, Ford, Reagan, Bush I, and Bush II. Republicans are wastrels.

Even the lionized CEO Jack Welch, the Republican former chief of General Electric, seems to have (though vaguely) sensed that Republicans had been bad even for the largest firms such as his. In the 8 March 2004 *BusinessWeek* (p. 78), Welch was asked "Is George Bush really good for Big Business?" (the question simply ignored *Small* Business), and he volunteered to address not only G.W. Bush but recent Presidents all the way back to Ronald Reagan, by saying: "The big myth is that George Bush is great for Big Business. I don't see this great connection. I never did, by the way. I never saw Ronald Reagan do it [benefit Big Business]. I never saw [Bush's] father do it. Without Bill Clinton, we wouldn't have had NAFTA. Without the North American Free Trade Agreement, we would have been really behind the eight ball in competitiveness." (He was correct there, but a Democratic version of NAFTA would have been even better, because it would have improved conditions for workers throughout North America, and wouldn't have skewed in favor of management and against labor. Welch didn't care about workers; he viewed things purely from the side of management.)

The economist Paul Krugman observed in his 27 February 2004 *New York Times* column: "Put it this way: there's a reason why the two U.S. presidents who did the most to promote growth in world trade were Franklin Roosevelt and Harry Truman, while the two most protectionist presidents of the last 70 years have been Ronald Reagan and, yes, George W. Bush." (The most protectionist of *all* presidents had actually left office just 72 years earlier: the Republican Herbert Hoover.)

Conservative so-called "libertarians" constantly accuse Democrats of being "protectionists," but the Smoot Hawley Tariff that helped to precipitate the Great Depression was a Republican initiative, *not* a Democratic one. And even the conservative *Wall Street Journal* editorialized, on 7 October 2005, criticizing "America's Bad Trade Example," and was seconding "Canada's deep dissatisfaction with the U.S. [read 'with President Bush's'] refusal to comply with multiple rulings that U.S. tariffs on Canadian softwood lumber violate the North American Free Trade Agreement (NAFTA)."

In May 1998, the Congressional Budget Office issued a study, *Long-Term Budgetary Pressures and Policy Options*, which opened, "The budget will be balanced this year for the first time since 1969." 1969 had been the end of an 8-year period of Democratic control of the White House. From 1969 onward, the bulk of the Vietnam War was waged, by Republican President Richard Nixon, who had promised that if elected he'd carry out a "secret plan to end the Vietnam War." His plan turned out to be bombing the enemy into submission. It didn't work. However, it started the federal deficits, which simply exploded under Ronald Reagan, and which were finally (though, sadly, only briefly) ended by Bill Clinton's 1993 upper-bracket tax-hikes, which Republicans said would turn out to be disastrous. They were wrong. (It's a *habit* of conservatives to be wrong, because conservative voters don't punish conservative politicians for being wrong. By contrast, progressive voters are strongly committed to accountability.)

Of course, the miserable economic performance of Republicans has been due to more than merely their protecting from foreign competition their corrupt financial backers. The entire conservative agenda is ultimately destructive of virtually the entire society. Only *corrupt* businesses derive short-term benefit from it, and conservative clergy derive the long-term benefit.

The neoliberal/neoconservative columnist at *The New York Times*, Thomas Friedman, headlined, on 22 April 2004, "Losing Our Edge?" and he warned, "The technology tide may be going out" in the U.S. He interviewed high-tech executives in Silicon Valley, and found that they were planning to ship many jobs overseas, where health care is paid by taxes, instead of by employers, and where better-educated workers are available at lower cost. "Anyone who thinks that all the Indian and Chinese techies are doing is answering call-center phones or solving tech problems for Dell customers is sadly mistaken." Decades of trickle-down economics in the U.S. were taking a toll upon the masses, for whom this trickling was little more than ignorance and poverty.

The religious prejudice in favor of Republicans being the party of entrepreneurs and business success, and being generally "good for business," was so strong that, in early March 2004, the very first of the Bush "re-"election campaign's TV commercials presented the 2001-2004 recession as if it had begun under President Bill Clinton (which is false: economists widely agree that it began under Bush himself), and presented President Bush as if he had pulled the nation out of that supposedly Democrat-generated slump. Such a bald lie wouldn't have succeeded at all if the American people had not been thoroughly indoctrinated into the myth that Democrats are bad for business, and that Republicans are good for business. While it's true that Republican deregulation caused the late-90's tech-boom to reach excessive bubble-proportions, this deregulation wasn't an initiative from a Democratic President, but from a Republican Congress. Democratic President Clinton did the best he could with the Republican Congress which was impeaching him. Only blind faith could cause any voter in 2004 to believe this TV commercial and to vote for the Republicans to get America's economy moving again.

And, in such a religious society, which therefore takes its beliefs upon the basis of *faith* in authority — instead of upon the basis of *findings* in science, such as have here been summarized — this Big Lie (that Republicans are good for the economy) has gone over big. Here's how pervasive this lie has been in the United States: On the afternoon of election day 2004, Reuters headlined "Blogs Send Stocks into Reverse," and reported, "U.S. stocks reversed course suddenly on Tuesday and drifted lower as chatter on the internet speculated that early exit polls had Sen. John Kerry leading the presidential election in key swing states." By contrast, early in the following afternoon, as Wall Street reacted to news of the Bush victory, Reuters headlined "Stocks Surge," and noted,

"The Dow Jones industrial average was up 137.84 points, or
1.37 percent." This was off the opening's high, when "The
Dow's gain of 1.7 percent matched its best one-day gain of the
year." A supposed market expert was quoted as saying
"Investors are happy" about Bush's win, because "he's put
through some favorable policies for investors." (This pundit
wouldn't even know what's good for investors, but enough of
them followed his advice so that such a comment helped raise
Bush's standing even further among them.) The investing
class were such fools that they actually believed that keeping
George W. Bush in office would be good for U.S. stock values!
But unfortunately, ugly reality intruded itself in the
background: buried at the end of the article was the
anomalous news that, "The election eclipsed earnings results,"
which were down, and that, "Meanwhile, a snap shot of the
U.S. economy showed new orders at U.S. factories dropped
unexpectedly" for the second month in a row. As the AP
reported, "Demand dropped sharply for all manufactured
goods except defense materials. It was the first back-to-back
monthly decline since November-December" almost a year
before. The Republican Fed chief Allan Greenspan, and the
Republican Administration, had propped this corpse up until
the election was over.

Three days after the election, *USA Today* headlined
"Election's Conclusion Sparks Market Rallies: Investors seem
pleased with Bush's growth agenda." Adam Shell reported:
"The so-called ownership society trumpeted by President
Bush is already reaping dividends from a big rally inspired by
the president's re-election. In the two trading days since the
election, the broad U.S. stock market, as measured by the
Standard & Poor's 500 index, has seen its value rise 3% and hit
a high for the year. ... It also added $350 billion to the value of
the stock market, according to Wilshire Associates." Lots of
people had faith in Republican misrule.

America was definitely a nation of faith, not of science.
Similarly (though in a different field, which was mentioned
before), a CBS News poll issued just weeks later, on

November 22nd, was headlined "Poll: Creationism Trumps Evolution" among the American public. In today's America, stock in the Bible was selling high, and stock in science was selling low. Faith clearly reigned, over science. Clergy, in their pulpits and TV and radio parishes, were encouraging faith-based — not systematically skeptical — beliefs, and were thereby preparing the minds of the masses of gullible Americans to believe the already scientifically exposed falsehood that "Republicans are good for business and Democrats are bad for business." When people have faith in a lie, they easily dismiss contrary evidence. Scientific findings are thus often ignored, in a religious society.

But this myth was, supposedly, secular, not "religious." Who, then, actually originated such a myth? Of course, the insiders, the aristocracy, did. Those who benefited from Republican misrule were the authorities in whom the exploited masses possessed faith about such "secular" matters. After all, these authorities, who had all "the right connections" — even if from birth, instead of from any personal achievements — were the people who knew what to do with money, weren't they? These were the big contributors to many churches. God had blessed them with success, and so they were the ones who must know what to do with money.

The owners of our major media also propagate this myth. Mortimer Zuckerman is one of the very few presslords who write his own editorials, and, in his *U.S. News & World Report*, on 21 March 2005, this proudly conservative owner of that conservative magazine, as well as of the conservative New York *Daily News,* (and the former owner of the conservative *The Atlantic*) editorialized in *U.S. News* about "The Case of the 12 Zeros," condemning the Republican Party, by saying, "We're looking at trillions in federal debt — and still the GOP wants more tax cuts and spending." He was a conservative Israel-at-all-costs Democrat who criticized the Republican Party for its squanderousness. But he often propagandized for Republicans, by hiring conservative

journalists. Here, he asserted that Republicans were "turning
their backs on the GOP's historical record of responsible fiscal
management." This assertion wasn't true at all: Bush was
instead merely recapitulating the bum fiscal record of
Republican Ronald Reagan, but with a vengeance.
Zuckerman's Wharton MBA couldn't help this mogul do the
adding and subtracting right, to calculate the Republican
Party's actual record. And his journalistic hires promulgated
the very same myths. For example, in the same issue of the
same magazine, one of Mr. Zuckerman's employees, Michael
Barone, headlined that "The Democrats Are Out of Gas," and
cited, in support of his opinion: "In the *New Republic*, John
Judis takes a longer view. Since the 1970s, he notes, Democrats
have had little success expanding government." If it's a lie to
assert that Democrats try to expand government while
Republicans try to reduce it, then it's also a lie to *imply* this;
Barone was simply lying.

The falsehood is promulgated also by "moderate
Republicans" — to the extent that any of them are still around.
For example, Richard S. Dunham headlined in *BusinessWeek*,
on 30 May 2005, "The GOP: Rainy Days For Blue-Sky
Thinking," and reported, with apparent regret, that
"Republican dreams of transforming America into a free-
enterprise bee-hive might be beyond their powers of political
persuasion." Would anyone refer, in such a way, to "Mafia
dreams of transforming Italy into a free-enterprise bee-hive"?
Evidently, Republicans' "powers of political persuasion" beat
the Mafia's – at least for him.

Similarly, the supposedly liberal NPR "reporter" Julie
Rovner opined on "Morning Edition," 21 September 2005,
"Democrats are trying to force additional spending that
Congress would otherwise be unlikely to approve." She
utterly ignored that this Republican Congress was the worst
porkbarrel Congress in U.S. history — and that the Democrats
in this Congress were, in any case, far from being in a position
"to force" anything there. What was actually at issue here was
a Republican initiative, in the wake of Hurricane Katrina, to

reduce Medicaid for the poor, and simultaneously to increase yet further the tax reductions for the wealthiest Americans. The real issue was fiscal priorities — not at all fiscal deficit as she implied. In fact, Republicans in Congress were spending enormous taxpayer funds on porkbarrel projects for their well-to-do constituents. But her report accepted uncritically House Republican allegations that slashes in Medicaid were necessary for fiscal discipline. She was implicitly championing: Take from the poor, to give to the rich. But she did it within the context of the Republican line: Democrats favor "big government," and Republicans favor "small government." The entire gist of her "news" was thus deceptive.

Mortimer Zuckerman's 22 May 2006 *USN&WR* editorial was headlined "Hypocrisy on Stilts," which was the phrase that he was applying to Republicans who "define themselves as fiscal conservatives after five years of profligacy." This conservative then proceeded to express outrage against Republicanism: "So, do our elected officials try to increase the minimum wage? No. Do they try to cut taxes for the poor or provide more medical care? No. What do they do? They give even more tax benefits to the wealthiest." Republicans were now down in the opinion polls, and Zuckerman needed to sell magazines; he dumped on Republicans. But he didn't fire and replace his journalistic staff, whose propaganda had helped to place Republicans into control of Washington. Nor did Zuckerman say anything to inform his readers that the Republican Party wasn't any more of a small-government party than the Nazis were, nor that the Democratic Party was actually *less* of a big-government party than the Republicans were. He wasn't out to disabuse his readers of such Republican myths against Democrats. But, at least now, he was no longer repeating his recent reference to "the GOP's historical record of responsible fiscal management." Without his apologizing for having stated that lie, he even acknowledged implicitly here that it was false, when he referred to the fiscal profligacy of Republican

President Ronald Reagan, by observing, "It doesn't help that Vice President Cheney is quoted as having said, 'Reagan proved deficits don't matter.'" Perhaps, when Zuckerman criticized his fellow-conservatives for "Hypocrisy on Stilts," he was actually criticizing himself most of all.

Another typical example of conservatives trumpeting a supposed big-government bent in the Democratic Party was the correspondent of National Public Radio (and, of course, Republicans constantly label NPR as "liberal"), Juan Williams, saying, on "Fox News Sunday," on 5 November 2006: "At the moment, most people are telling pollsters that they trust the Democrats more on taxes than they do the Republicans. To me, that's crazy." Perhaps the high-income Mr. Williams didn't know that average and poor Americans had experienced no "tax cut" at all from the Republican President and Congress; perhaps he simply didn't care whether or not they had. But to call "crazy" what actually made entirely good sense, was, in either case, unprofessional journalism.

Another typical example was a 29 November 2005 op-ed in the *Wall Street Journal*, by former Republican House Majority Leader, Dick Armey, headlined "It's My Party: Why Are Republican Leaders Governing Like Democrats?" (He was asking this while House Republicans were cutting food stamps and Medicaid to pay for yet more top-bracket tax cuts, and while Democrats were united in opposing this Republican proposal.) Armey opened one key paragraph by saying, "As the party of smaller government, Republicans …," which was the popular but false assumption.

And Justin Fox, "The Curious Capitalist" in *TIME*, headlined on 18 February 2008, "Do Presidents Matter? It's not clear that the White House can change the economy." Mr. Fox said: "Over the past half-century, Democratic administrations have seen faster economic growth — and better stock-market performance — than Republican ones. But the sample size is so small that you really can't rule out luck." So, "In search of more clarity, I called Jim Leach, the former Republican Congressman from Iowa who has long had a reputation as one of Capitol Hill's deepest thinkers." (Leach had actually been co-author of the notorious Gramm-Leach Bliley Act in 1999, which repealed FDR's anti conflict-of-interest banking laws. Leach was thus partly to blame for George W. Bush's U.S. mortgage-meltdown and economic collapse.) "Do Presidents matter to the economy? I asked. 'In normal times they modestly matter. In abnormal times — and this is abnormal — they matter a great deal,' said Leach, currently director of the Institute of Politics at Harvard's Kennedy School of Government." So, there you have it, from one of "Capitol Hill's deepest thinkers": Only "In abnormal times" does the (actually massive) statistical record indicate that Democratic Presidents are superior to Republican Presidents, for the nation's economy. And we were also told here that this has been true only "Over the past half-century," which meant *post*-Eisenhower, *starting* with JFK. It supposedly *wasn't* true, for example, in regards to Truman, FDR, Hoover, and Harding.

With such mythologizing being routine among the "news" reporters and commentators in America's major "news" media, how can the American people *not* be fooled?

On 21 August 2006, the "libertarian" The Independent Institute came forth with a "Policy Report" by Winslow T. Wheeler, who had recently worked as a staffer for Republican Senator Pete Domenici on the Senate Budget Committee. Titled "Congress, the Defense Budget and Pork," Wheeler's report said that over his 31-year Capitol Hill career, "I have observed 'pork' add-ons to defense bills evolve from a sometime-activity that professional staff members would deride — but sometimes engage in — to an activity aggressively pursued by virtually all, occupying vast amounts of work time. ... In choosing between pork or fully funding wartime basics (such as training for the troops, their food and everyday supplies, maintenance to repair worn out weapons, and spare parts to keep them running on the battlefield), Congress has clearly opted to lard on the pork to skimp on soldiers' basics." Wheeler spoke of the showboating of

Republican Senator John McCain, a permanent candidate for
President: "At the end of his 'pork buster' speech, he usually
sits down or leaves the Senate chamber, doing nothing
further." Also, during one wave of "reform," Republican
Senators Trent Lott and Susan Collins came up with a bill,
which was "a sham." What finally passed was McCain's
"Pork-Barrel Reduction Act," which "achieves nothing more
than different plumbing: The underlying reality doesn't
change. ... McCain's 'reforms' were not as utterly transparent
as the Lott/Collins bill; McCain's ideas were far more clever:
They appeared to bring real change, but in fact brought little."
Wheeler said that any *authentic* change would entail "an
independent estimate of the cost" of any earmark; "An
evaluation by the Government Accountability Office ... on the
effectiveness and appropriateness of the proposed spending";
and, "A requirement that any earmark ... can only be awarded
to a contractor after complete and open nation-wide contract
competition." However, of course, any proposal like that
wouldn't serve the purpose that the Gingrich/DeLay/Armey
team had established, of keeping Republican Party campaign
coffers brim-full of cash. The Party's only constituencies were
executives of large corporations, and of large evangelical
Christian organizations. Pork was the Republican way to win,
and that's why it blossomed during Republican Congresses
under Republican Presidents.

   Incidentally, not only do large U.S. firms
overwhelmingly favor the Republican over the Democratic
Party, but large foreign firms also do. The website
www.opensecrets.org/pacs/foreign.php "Foreign-Connected
PACs" showed that more than 95% of the Political Action
Committees of foreign firms in the U.S. favored the
Republican over the Democratic Party, and by about the same
overwhelming ratios as did domestic U.S. firms' PAC's,
typically by about two-to-one or higher ratios. In the money-
race, the Democratic Party had never been able to compete
with the Republican Party, at least not for over a hundred
years. Any corrupt entity will tend to prefer a conservative

government, and the vast majority of successful firms are corrupt — that's how most of them *became* successful.

On 24 March 2007 David Cay Johnston headlined in *The New York Times*, "Foreigners Get Benefit of Tax Cut," and he reported that, "A 2003 tax cut that President Bush promoted as a way to create jobs in the United States includes a provision that has given some foreign companies a financial advantage over their American competitors. ... It can cost an American company as much as $540 million more than a foreign company to pay $1 billion to United States investors. The administration has generally kept silent about this advantage, which was widely known in tax circles." Foreign companies had gotten more than their money's worth out of the Republicans.

After Democrats swept a lot of the Republican trash out of Congress in the November 2006 elections, and took control, the Republican *Wall Street Journal* grudgingly headlined an editorial "Earmark Victory" and announced that Senate Republicans (who were now the minority) "could do worse than to build on this week's Senate earmark victory." which was passed on a 98-to-0 vote in the now Democratic-controlled Senate. These fascist editors said that the bill had passed (after what had actually been the long night of Republican control of Congress since 1994) because "Senate Democrats did an about-face and jumped on the earmark-reform bandwagon," as if the Republican majority in the Senate had been opposing earmarks when they controlled the Senate and when Republicans also controlled the House. (Republicans had entered the majority in Congress in 1994 promising to eliminate corruption, but promptly put into place operations geared to escalate corruption and to punish the major contributors to the Democratic Party.) "More amazing was Democrats' new enthusiasm for oversight," which Democrats had *actually* been *pleading for*, during their long hiatus from power. "Republicans made headlines with their demands last week, and the news stories were a welcome change for a public appalled by Congress's spend-

happy ways." Had these editorialists attended the Joseph
Goebbels Institute, to learn their craft, or did they learn it in
the cradle? To read this editorial, one would think that, after a
long period of Democratic control, Congress had finally
switched to Republican control in November 2006, except for
the editorial's incongruous opening: "If Republicans are
wondering how best to shorten their time in the minority, they
could do worse than to build on this week's Senate earmark
victory." Oh, it was a *Republican* victory? Not a victory by
Democrats *against* Republicans? What was actually happening
during the 1994-2006 period, when earmarks skyrocketed?

On 30 March 2007, *The New York Times* featured an op-
ed by Thomas Schatz, identified as "the president of Citizens
Against Government Waste, a nonprofit group in
Washington." The headline was "Pork Goes to War," and his
article castigated the Democratic Congress for having "used
pork to buy votes" so as to pass a spending bill which would
establish a time-limit upon America's military occupation of
Iraq. Schatz listed 52 of the budgeted programs as being
especially outrageous, the smallest of which was $2 million,
and the largest of which was $1.25 billion. The largest, the
$1.25 billion item, was for "Public housing agencies" (not
identified further by Mr. Schatz, nor were any of the others
listed by him) which Republicans had cut, and which
Democrats evidently thought deserved more funding. Did Mr.
Schatz have to display his conservatism so baldly as this? The
next-biggest of the 52 items was $969.65 million, nearly $1
billion, for "Influenza pandemic preparedness," a national-
security necessity which the Republican Congress had shorted
and which Democrats, again, believed deserved and needed
more funding. The third-biggest item, at $750 million, was
"State Children's Health Insurance Fund," and a corrupt
Republican Party that received scads of campaign cash from
commercial health insurers wasn't likely to favor this item
either, and didn't, but was it necessarily "pork"? He offered
no reason to believe it to be. He simply assumed that any
assistance to American families to help their children keep

their health constituted "pork." Perhaps such an expense on children's healthcare would greatly reduce America's future overall healthcare costs and turn out to be highly efficient, but Schatz simply *assumed* that it's "pork." The fourth-biggest item, at $660 million, was "Transportation Security Administration for purchase of an explosives detection system," which was widely viewed as being one of the most important unfunded national security necessities, and which the Republican Congress and President had ignored. The fifth-biggest item was $640 million for "Low Income Home Energy Assistance Program" (commonly known by its acronym, LIHEAP) which was a long-established and much appreciated program to assist poor people in northern states to heat their homes during the winter.

These items were "pork" in the eyes of Republicans.

The Republican Party's corrupt priorities might help to explain why the U.S. economy consistently performs better under Democratic than under Republican administrations.

Sourcewatch.com's article on "Citizens Against Government Waste" asserts that this organization "has campaigned on behalf of the tobacco industry and in favor of Microsoft and against open source software." (Both of those were solid right-wing positions.) CAGW "was founded in 1984 by [the hard-Right Republican heir to a chemical fortune] J. Peter Grace (1913-1995) and Jack Anderson." "The conservative Capital Research Center [which is a fee-accessed site] notes in its Searchlight database (which records corporate and general foundation contributions) that CAGW has 'received funding from: Lynde and Harry Bradley Foundation, Merrill Lynch & Company Foundation, Exxon Corporation (now ExxonMobil), Ingersol-Rand Company, Johnson & Johnson, F.M. Kirby Foundation, Philip Morris, RJR Nabisco (now part of the Altria Group), Sears Roebuck & Company." All of these were movement-conservative entities, and each of them had made substantial financial contributions to CAGW, and overwhelmingly to the Republican and not to the Democratic Party. Furthermore, no Democrat was among

CAGW's Directors. One Director, Vin Weber, had been a Republican Congressman. Another was a member of the Grace family. A letter dated "January 22, 2007" was posted to the internet headlined "TAKE A STAND AGAINST TAX INCREASES ON WORKING FAMILIES AND AMERICAN BUSINESSES," urging people to write to Congress in support of the Republican position on taxes and spending, and asserting that, "the threat to American taxpayers and businesses is real as the actions of the new [Democratic] House leadership in the past week signal their desire to raise taxes." It was signed by 34 organizations, all hard-Right, including Club for Growth, Americans for Tax Reform (Grover Norquist's organization, which was started by the Reagan White House), Christian Coalition, Eagle Forum (Phyllis Schlafly's group), ... and, of course, CAGW.

When The New York Times published this op-ed, without indicating that it was corporate-paid propaganda parading in the *NYT* as journalistic opinion, this newspaper was being entirely consistent with its history as a propaganda-vehicle for the agenda of conservative aristocrats. Furthermore, instead of CAGW having had to pay to place this propaganda in the *NYT* as an advertisement, Mr. Schatz was paid by *NYT* an author's fee in order for it to appear in the newspaper as an opinion-piece. This newspaper, in effect, paid CAGW to advertise in it. That's how far-Right this "liberal" newspaper really is.

However, even CAGW had to admit that as soon as Democrats took over Congress after 2006, earmarks plunged. CAGW's chart, "Pork-Barrel Spending, 1995 to 2008," showed that the figure rose during each year of Bush's Presidency, to $29 billion in 2006, and then fell off the cliff, suddenly to $13.2 billion in 2007. There still remained cause for concern, but the problem was greatly reduced. For example, on 8 June 2008, the AP headlined "Earmark Beneficiaries Help Benefactors' Re-Election," and reported eight instances where earmarked funds correlated with very large contributions to the congressperson's re-election campaign. Three of the eight examples were Republicans; five were Democrats — perhaps control of Congress gave Democrats the edge, but the total amount of pork still was down significantly from the prior years of Republican control.

Furthermore, the myth that Republicans are good for investors isn't generated merely by such Republican-owned media and their think tanks. It has always had its propagandists and True Believers also in academia, people whose careers have been financed by the very worst aristocrats — the aristocrats who take advantage of their inside positions so as to sell what faithful suckers will eagerly buy. Some of these scholar/propagandists have even gone on to win Nobel prizes in economics, for other work they've done that's less seedy than such shilling for the aristocracy.

One example was the economist Gary Becker from the University of Chicago and Stanford's Hoover Institution, the latter of which institution was named, appropriately, for the Republican U.S. President (Herbert Hoover) who helped to bring on the Great Depression, culminating twelve straight years of Republican misrule with the Big Crash. So, Becker represented the very people who caused the Great Depression — no wonder he wasn't a Democrat! Writing in the 12 January 2004 *BusinessWeek* (p. 26), this ceaseless scholarly propagandist for the Republican Party had the nerve to predict — despite all history, and all economic evidence — that "The much-criticized Bush tax cuts will definitely help the economy grow more rapidly in the longer run." He simply ignored the inevitable impact which those cuts would have on the federal deficit, and on future interest rates. Typical of such conservative fantasizers, he was committed to the false view that governmental deficits result *only* from too much money departing from the government in spending, never at all from too little money coming into it through taxes. He simply blotted out the income side of the federal ledger. And he also didn't attribute the huge Bush deficits to too little, and wrong, governmental investments in infrastructure, education, etc. This professional economist had no sense of fiscal mismanagement. He, in fact, ignored Bush's deficits altogether. Dr. Becker's prediction of a Bush boom was nothing more than an election-year fraud, which exhibited how ruthlessly such True Believers will occasionally propagandize for their frauds. This fantasist went on, from that shoddy base, to predict that the U.S. economy, under Bush, would create a global boom by Bush's tax cuts boosting demand from U.S. consumers (who were actually being impoverished by Republican trickle-down economics — it didn't trickle). In other words, Bush, who was bleeding the poor to feed the rich, and rubber-stamping the worst pork-barrel Congress in U.S. history, would supposedly generate a surge in demand from those drained, depressed, U.S. consumers. What nonsense! The only consumers who were net benefiting from Bush's policies were the top 1%. So, this Nobelist was actually implying that U.S. demand comes predominantly from that 1%, the tiny fraction of the wealthiest Americans, the small number of net beneficiaries from Bush's tax cuts and corruption. Dr. Becker was himself one of these fortunate people, a beneficiary from those corrupt policies and people, and (as an authentic conservative) he would not betray his benefactors, no matter what the truth was.

Even after seven years of Bush's economic disaster, the *Wall Street Journal* on 11 January 2008 headlined "Odds of Recession Seen Rising" and yet reported that of 54 economists who were polled, 59% chose "A Republican president" and only 28% chose "A Democratic president" when asked "Do you think the stock market would perform better under ... ?" To call economics a "science" under that condition is ludicrous, like calling physics a "science" before Galileo, when to acknowledge a non-geocentric universe was blasphemy. Economics hasn't yet seen its Galileo. What those professional economists were saying here was in direct contradiction of the overwhelming and consistent empirical record on the subject, an empirical finding which is among the most firmly established — if not actually the most firmly established of all

— empirical findings yet, anywhere throughout all of the social sciences.

In a religious society, beliefs are taken largely on faith, and therefore these constantly reinforced prejudices become self-perpetuating. Consequently, when 145 big-corporate CFO's were polled by *CFO* magazine in September 2004 (p. 48), the magazine reported that "finance executives favor the President over his Democratic challenger by 71 percent to 28 percent. And 75 percent think Bush will be better than Kerry for their businesses." With that ratio of Republicans, this group might as well have been composed of 100% Christian fundamentalists, or else 100% top one-percenters. But perhaps some of these CFO's were merely corrupt, in which case their preference for Bush wasn't insane after all. Certainly, any who were *not* corrupt and who favored Bush, might as well have *been* insane: this President was the worst fiscal disaster in U.S. history; and yet regardless, conservatives of all stripes were infatuated with him: he won 90% of their votes.

The 16 April 2007 *New York* headlined "The Running of the Hedgehogs" about hedge fund managers, and reported that a recent survey of that elite group showed that, "60.5% are registered Republicans" and "28.6% are registered Democrats."

The very same conservatives were predicting gloom and doom when Democrat Bill Clinton beat George H.W. Bush in 1992, and most of these conservatives even today refuse to acknowledge that their predictions then turned out to be wildly wrong. One of the few conservatives who did finally recognize publicly the economic success of the Clinton Presidency was Bruce Bartlett, who had worked in the Reagan White House and then at the U.S. Treasury under the senior President Bush. In a *New York Times* op-ed on 1 July 2004, this Republican headlined, concerning the Clinton period, "Those Were the Days," and he admitted, frankly, "Like most conservatives, I thought Bill Clinton was a terrible president when he was in office," but that "conservatives should rethink the Clinton presidency." He then proceeded to explain:

"Bringing the federal budget into surplus is obviously an achievement. After inheriting a deficit of 4.7 percent of gross domestic product in 1992 [due partly to Mr. Bartlett's own conservative policies], Mr. Clinton turned this into a surplus of 2.4 percent of G.D.P. in 2000 — a remarkable turnaround. ... By contrast, Mr. Clinton's Republican successor has caused the surplus to evaporate, raised total federal spending by 1.6 percent of G.D.P., established a new entitlement program for prescription drugs and adopted the most protectionist trade policy since Herbert Hoover." However, even Mr. Bartlett couldn't admit that the achievements of the Clinton Presidency were due to the extent to which it was progressive not conservative, and that the problem with both of the Bush Presidencies was their rank conservatism. Instead, Bartlett went on to allege that, "Mr. Clinton accomplished conservative objectives against his will in some cases, and in others only because a Republican Congress prevented him from enacting more liberal reforms." Bartlett, who had been brainwashed into conservative myths, simply couldn't let go of them, no matter what. More accurate would have been for him to have observed, for example, that President Clinton's healthcare program was actually too conservative to have been able to succeed (for example, it wasn't a single-payer system), yet was still too liberal to have been able to pass in the reactionary Newt Gingrich Republican Congress. Mr. Bartlett couldn't bring himself to admit that the problem with conservatism is conservatism — *not* liberalism, much less progressivism.

On 18 February 2009, daggatt.blogspot.com headlined "The 1993 Budget Act," and opened:

"On August 10, 1993, President Clinton signed into law the Omnibus Budget Reconciliation Act of 1993 (the 1993 Budget Act). Four days earlier, it had passed the Senate by a vote of 51 to 50 – with Vice President Gore breaking a tie and casting the deciding 51st vote for passage. (Note: You didn't have to get 60 votes to pass anything in the Senate in those days. The filibuster was reserved for extraordinary occasions, like denying civil rights to black people.) The day before that it had passed the House by a vote of 218 to 216. In both Houses of Congress, the vote literally could not have been closer. And in both cases, not a single Republican voted in support of the Act."

Following that piece of history was a summary of this tax-law's provisions, which removed the Reagan/(G.H.W.)Bush upper-bracket tax-cuts; and then a series of quotations was presented, from immediately prior to this Act's passage, in which Newt Gingrich, Bob Michel, John Kasich, Bob Dornan, Chris Cox, Phil Crane, Dick Armey, Jim Ramstad, Jim Bunning, and other leading Republicans of the 1990's, condemned this then-proposed legislation, by saying such things as "It will slow economic growth, contribute to the massive federal deficit." All of these Republican predictions turned out to be the exact opposite of what actually happened in the Act's wake. Republicans should have simply been hounded out of government after this; they had now proven, yet again, their outrageous unreliability on economic matters; but instead, they remained in office and continued making more false predictions, not just during the Clinton Administration prior to President George W. Bush, but even throughout Democratic President Barack Obama's Administration which came after Bush. The market for Republican garbage still remained strong; there still remained millions of conservative dupes in America.

Academicians and Republicans can find excuses for Republican squanderousness (such as by blaming Democrats), but they never excuse Democratic squanderousness when that occurs. On 8 September 2005, commentator David Wessel headlined in the *Wall Street Journal*, "Small-Government Rhetoric Gets Filed Away [in the wake of Hurricane Katrina]," and he opened: "The era of small government is over. Sept. 11 challenged it. Katrina killed it." However, this excuse for Bush and the Republican Congress's wastefulness was actually a bald lie; George W. Bush and his Republican Congress were wastrels even *prior* to 9/11, and their porkbarrel spending programs dwarfed 9/11 costs. Furthermore, the invasion/occupation of Iraq ended up costing far more than did that of Afghanistan — the *authentic* anti-terrorism war — and created terrorists instead of reducing them; and so, Republicans were *hyper*-wasteful, even in their military endeavors. Wessel continued his fraud by quoting a scholar who shared it: "'The era of big government wasn't over,' says Allen Schick, a professor of public policy at the University of Maryland. 'Look what happened with spending. It was hibernating under Clinton and revived under Bush.' ... Katrina already is adding fuel to the spending fire. 'Democrats will spend because they love to spend and Republicans will spend because they have to,' Mr. Schick says." Evidently, it didn't strike Dr. Schick that spending's having "hibernated" under Democrats, who supposedly "love to spend," while spending "revived" under Republicans, who supposedly are reluctant to spend, *simply doesn't compute*. It contradicts itself. Any professor of public policy who promulgates the lie that the Republican Party is less — rather than *more* — inclined to squander taxpayers' money than is the Democratic Party, should be exposed as the fraud/propagandist he is: Such a person may be a scholar, but he's no scientist; he's just another person of faith.

Republican politicians are assiduous to perpetuate this myth. Not only did the Heritage Foundation and other Republican Party podiums decry loudly George W. Bush's abysmal fiscal record and claim that it violated — rather than epitomized — fiscal management by conservatives, but Republican politicians also pontificated against Bush's deficits, even though these very same conservatives had, in fact, legislated and rammed through these very same budgets and tax-cuts which had produced the deficits. (Indeed, their having passed the President's proposals was a key reason why President Bush, unlike all other presidents, didn't veto a single bill until his July 2006 veto of stem-cell research.) Thus, on 13 March 2006, *The New York Times* headlined "Budget Restraint Emerges As G.O.P. Theme for 2008," and reported that, "As prospective Republican presidential candidates search for themes to distinguish their prospective campaigns, and distance themselves from the embattled incumbent in the White House, they appear to be in agreement on what one central issue should be in 2008: Curbing the federal spending that has soared under President Bush." It was as if Germany's Nazi Party were to have condemned anti-Semitism after having exterminated every Jew in the world — supreme political hypocrisy. Conservatives are simply corrupt to the core.

Democrats Reduce, Republicans Grow, Government Deficits

Here's the actual record on deficits, under the various recent Presidents:

According to the wikipedia article on "National Debt by U.S. Presidential Terms," the column "Increase debt/GDP (in percentage points)" shows that under Democrat FDR's final term, 1941-45, when the U.S. was waging WWII, the debt soared 67.1%. During Democrat Truman's first term, 1945-49, it declined 24.4%. During Truman's second term, 1949-53, it declined 21.7%. During Republican Ike's first term, 1953-57, it declined 11.0%. During Ike's second term, it declined 5.2%. During the Democrat Kennedy/Johnson term, it declined 8.3%. During Johnson's second term, it again declined 8.3%. During Republican Nixon's first term, 1969-73, it declined 3.0%. During the Nixon/Ford term, it rose 0.2% – the first rise since WWII. During Democrat Carter's one term, 1977-81, it again declined, this time by 3.3%. Then, in came Republican Reagan (whom opinion polls that have been taken after the year 2000 show that Republican voters consider to have been the greatest President of all time), and in his first term, 1981-85, it soared upward, 11.3%. In Reagan's second term, it again soared, this time by 9.3%. During Republican George H.W. Bush's term, 1989-93, it soared even more, 13.0%. During Democrat Clinton's first term, 1993-97, it declined 0.7%. In his second term, it again declined, 9.0%. During Republican

George W. Bush's first term, 2001-05, it again rose, 7.1%.
During his second term, it soared, 20.7%.

Deficits really started with Ronald Reagan, who
slashed top-bracket taxes during peacetime and thereby
deprived the federal coffers of essential income, with the
resulting deficits all going onto the nation's credit card as a
problem for future generations to deal with.

The economist Satyajit Das wrote in 2011 about "The
Problem of US Debt," and he said: "Between 1981 and 1989,
tax cuts and peacetime defense spending contributed to an
increase in the debt of $1.9 trillion. [When Reagan had entered
office, the entire federal debt was only $1 trillion; he nearly
tripled it, during peacetime. His Presidency was a fiscal
disaster.] ... Under President George Bush Senior, the national
debt increased another $1.5 trillion. ... Under President Bill
Clinton, national debt increased $1.4 trillion [but GDP soared
vastly more]. ... Between 2001 and 2009, President George
Bush Junior added $6.1 trillion in debt [he doubled it]."
America was now a nation that was soaring its debt *during
peacetime*. Republican Presidents, and Republican congresses,
were destroying the country, by Republican corruption.

And yet Republicans have the nerve to preach fiscal
austerity to everyone except the aristocracy. And this
Republican hoax is constantly assumed and promoted in the
nation's "news" media. Except for Obama (the fake
"Democrat" who oversaw George W. Bush's third Presidential
term), all Democrats were better than all Republicans, when it
came to not burdening future generations with adding debt to
pay for the excesses and outright crimes of today's aristocracy.

Even on a local level, Republicans tend to be bad for the
economy, because they're the conservative party and so —
following from their Tribal and Religious values — they tend
to be corrupt. Typical was the case of New York's Long Island,
comprising two counties: Nassau and Suffolk. On 10
November 2005, *The New York Times* headlined "Democrats
Gain on Long Island, a Onetime G.O.P. Bastion," and
explained: "The catalyst in Nassau County was the

Republican mismanagement that left the county in a serious fiscal crisis, even during the economic boom of the late 1990's. Voters revolted. In Suffolk County, Republicans were implicated in a series of scandals — some referred to Brookhaven as 'Crookhaven' — leaving many voters disenchanted with the local Republican Party and ready for a change." Then, on Friday, 10 March 2006, the *Times* headlined "Day After Quitting Islip Post, A G.O.P. Stalwart Pleads Guilty," and reported: "Peter McGowan, the Islip town supervisor and once one of the most powerful Republicans on Long Island, pleaded guilty on Thursday to charges of accepting thousands of dollars of kickbacks and stealing from his campaign fund to pay for restaurant meals, vacations and visits to spas."

Another example was the very Republican County of San Diego in California, a military base. In 2006, its Republican congressman Randy "Duke" Cunningham went to prison for having long solicited and lived high from bribes paid by military contractors. Also, on September 27th of that year, the very Republican *Wall Street Journal* editorialized about "San Diego and the SEC" and noted that, "San Diego is approaching the bitter end of its pension-fund scandal. ... But the nightmare won't end there for San Diego taxpayers, who are left holding the bag for the malfeasance of the city council." Unusual for a large city, San Diego was predominantly Republican. Its government was larded with officials who were caught taking bribes. In such a corrupt culture, the public-sector unions can hardly be expected to remain clean. "San Diego's pension fund is now under-funded by some $1.5 billion, or about 30%. ... Michael Aguirre, the pugnacious city attorney, has brought suit in federal court to have some of the benefits granted since 1996 rolled back on grounds that they violated federal conflict-of-interest laws. A self-described liberal Democrat, Mr. Aguirre deserves kudos for risking the wrath of the public-sector unions." The conservative voters of San Diego County and City had left a heritage of fiscal squalor. However, voters weren't as much to blame as they were themselves victims: local elections were often corrupt, and the Republican Party tended to run vote-counting.

The era of Democratic corruption, such as of Tammany Hall and of the Dixiecrats, is increasingly in the past, not in the present, even less in the future, because a central conservative theme has always encouraged corruption, and the era of Democratic Party conservatism is long past. This conservative theme is that government in a democracy is naturally corrupt — only the Kingdom of God is not corrupt (and sinful). Because America's conservatives are now virtually all Republicans, corruption has become something of a Republican specialty. It's "the free market." And the Law (man-made, in the Constitution; not God-made, in the Bible) is "regulation." Thus, Republican politicians *embody* their philosophy of government, by *being* corrupt. Democratic politicians do not. A corrupt Democratic politician is a fake Democrat (usually tribal). But a corrupt Republican politician is an authentic Republican.

[BOX]

From: **http://oversight.house.gov/story.asp?ID=1081**

Federal Government Red Tape Soaring
Under Medicare Prescription Drug Plan

Tuesday, July 18, 2006 -- A new study released by Reps. Henry A. Waxman and Stephen F. Lynch shows that the federal paperwork burden has grown to record levels under the Bush Administration, with the new Medicare prescription drug program adding over 200 million hours of government red tape.

The Medicare Prescription Drug program increased the paperwork load by 224 million hours, or 10 hours per enrollee.

Over the last five years, total government paperwork has grown to 8.7 billion hours per year. This is 1.3 billion more hours of government paperwork than in the final year of the Clinton Administration. This year, the average adult in the United States will spend almost an entire work week (39 hours) filling out [federal] government paperwork.

Statutory changes promoted by President Bush and enacted by Congress are major causes of the increased paperwork burden. Over half the increase in paperwork from 2004 -- 224 million hours -- is attributable to the complicated new Medicare prescription drug program. This is equivalent to approximately 10 hours of government paperwork for every person enrolled in the Medicare drug plan. Tax law changes and other recent legislation have also added hundreds of millions of hours of new government paperwork.

[end box]

Even Democratic policy successes tend to be corruptly credited instead to Republicans. For example, President Clinton's welfare-reform plan was often credited to the Newt Gingrich Republican Congress, simply because Republicans had long made political hay by saying that "welfare queens" were the big drain down which were pouring the tax dollars of hard-working Americans. Attacking welfare was Republican policy, because Republicans hate programs that serve the poor. (Actually, however, the majority of rip-offs from Medicaid and other programs for the poor was by doctors and healthcare corporations which overbilled the government, and not by recipients.) But finally, Jason DeParle in 2004 came out with his *American Dream: Three Women, Ten Kids and a Nation's Drive to End Welfare*. This book opened by describing how Arkansas Governor Bill Clinton came up with his national welfare-reform plan during 1991, after an intensive process of analyzing not just policies but also political focus groups, to design candidate Clinton's platform to win the Democratic nomination for the U.S. Presidency.

Then, on 23 August 2006, Robert Rector risked his post at the Republican Heritage Foundation by headlining at the website of the Washington Post, "Bill Clinton Was Right: He Saw the Roots of America's Welfare Problem." It's interesting that editors at the *Washington Post* didn't see fit to publish this amazing piece as an op-ed, but perhaps part of the reason was indicated by the essay's opening: "As a conservative analyst who spent much of the 1990s working against most of Bill Clinton's agenda — including even some aspects of his welfare reform proposals — it pains me to say this. Bill Clinton was right. He deserves more credit for the passage of welfare reform than most conservatives probably care to admit." Rector cited there DeParle's book as having opened his eyes to this "more credit," but then proceeded to ignore what DeParle documented, and to assert instead that, "No, Clinton didn't play a major role in shaping the policy details of the landmark 1996 act. ... It took a Republican Congress to translate Clinton's rhetoric into reality." Rector, perhaps in order to keep his job, ignored how President Clinton, confident that a Republican-dominated Congress would be committing political suicide if it refused to pass welfare reform into law, had demanded that provisions be included in the bill which would provide the carrots, and not only the sticks, which would succeed at getting welfare mothers not just to leave, but to stay off of, welfare. But even the concession that Rector made in this unpublished essay was courageous under the circumstances: His paychecks came from the fascists, and the nation's "news" media were heavily slanted to present Republican gangsters in the most favorable light possible. President Clinton made certain that welfare mothers would not be abandoned by the Federal Government but would instead be assisted, via child care and education, to obtain work so as to become self-sufficient. He achieved this despite — and not because of — a Republican Congress.

Republicans Actually Win by Punishing the Nation

Despite the Republican Party's dismal fiscal and economic record of conservatism, Republicans have won the White House far more frequently than have Democrats. People such as Wessel and Schick keep the myths alive that sustain the conservative gang and that place them into the White House and other elective offices. Ever since the Civil Rights Act of 1964, the long-term U.S. political trend has been Republican, even though Republicans have had such miserable economic records for such a long time. A religious country brings on the punishment, and just keeps asking for more. The biggest disease of a religious society is this absence of accountability. During the Religious Age, the cash spent by aristocrats promoting Republican myths always dwarfs the amount spent promoting Democratic truths (such as that Democrats in office are good for business), and so the conservative lies and distortions win out politically. It's as if the truth doesn't really make any difference to people who have been raised to *respect* faith. Furthermore, the religious outlook, faith — and the institution of clergy maintaining it — is constantly laying the foundation for public acceptance of those conservative lies and distortions ("It's God's will"). This is especially so, because each Sunday morning the underlying might-makes-right ethical system of worshipping the personification of power, The Almighty, is reinforced for millions of prospective voters; religion sets people up to have faith in conservative myths. That — and *not* science, which shows the *contrary* — is *why* this economic myth persists.

Taking advantage of this widespread prejudice in a religious society, the ultra-religious President Bush ran a barrage of false and misleading commercials during his 2004 election campaign, which presented his opponent, the Democrat John Kerry, as being (among other things) a threat to the nation's economy. Even the conservative, pro-Iraq-war, *Washington Post* was struck by and opposed these falsehoods, and headlined boldly, "From Bush, Unprecedented

Negativity: Scholars Say Campaign Is Making History With Often-Misleading Attacks." This article reported, "Scholars and political strategists say the ferocious Bush assault on Kerry this spring has been extraordinary both for the volume of attacks and for the liberties the president and his campaign have taken with the facts. ... Bush so far has aired 49,050 negative ads in the top 100 markets, or 75 percent of his advertising. Kerry has run 13,336 negative ads — or 27 percent of his total." Republicans win not by serving the public below, but by serving The Almighty above, behind which screen stand actually the biggest gangsters: the aristocracy.

The old theocratic religious way has never really permitted a booming economy to develop over any extended period of time. The simple truth is that the only people who have been benefiting from it have been the crooks at the top, the insiders: the aristocrats. The masses have suffered. That's the raw historical fact, which the respectable gangsters, their shills, and their suckers — *all three* kinds of Republicans — simply deny.

One great irony in all this is that even *honest* top-one-percenters, people of enormous wealth, end up suffering from the corruption of the Republican gang. The insiders aren't necessarily always the richest people; sometimes, extremely wealthy individuals are honest, and these people, too, suffer from the policies of the aristocratic/theocratic gang. A case-in-point was published on 29 July 2004: David Cay Johnston headlined in *The New York Times* "I.R.S. Says Americans' Income Shrank for 2 Consecutive Years," and he reported that "The overall income Americans reported to the government shrank for two consecutive years after the Internet stock market bubble burst in 2000." He noted that the plunge in incomes of "particularly those at the upper end of the spectrum, was much more severe" than the drop for average Americans.

For example, while almost all income-groups below $200,000/year were unaffected by the bursting of the tech-stock bubble, because those people held so little corporate stock, all income-groups *above* that level were hit hard, and the group that was hit the hardest of all were those who had earned more than $10 million per year: their incomes, on average, plunged 63.4% during this two-year period, 2001 and 2002.

This precipitous fall in the stock market might not have happened if only the Clinton Administration had succeeded in getting its anti-corruption initiatives passed in the U.S. Congress, and if only the Republican-sponsored energy-deregulation scheme that ultimately enriched Enron and impoverished California had not been passed, and if only – if only. At the end of the business-cycle, stocks go down, but this stock-plunge would have been far less than it was, if only aristocrats (in the Business Roundtable, United States Chamber of Commerce, and otherwise), and the Republicans in Congress, hadn't succeeded at blocking the Clinton Administration's efforts to clean up corporate reporting, and to achieve more honest and democratic corporate governance, and more honest regulation.

Only the aristocratic crooks won out from what the Republicans did. This is also the reason why the honest big-business faction, the Committee for Economic Development, were pressing so hard for campaign finance reform, and were even willing to antagonize the gangsters' Party in order to be able to reduce the gangsters' competitive advantages against all decent people.

Bush's drive for "the free market" was actually only a drive to empower corporate crooks, and this placed honest businesspeople at a competitive disadvantage. The 3 September 2007 *BusinessWeek* featured several reports documenting this. "'Expect Lots More Embarrassment': Master dealmaker Bruce Wasserstein provides some much needed perspective on the current turmoil," presented Mr. Wasserstein responding to the question "What do you see as the underlying causes of this market convulsion?" by his saying: "Part of it is related to the lack of transparency in many of these assets. The regulators and rating agencies also allowed piling risk upon risk. Financial institutions spread the risk to people who weren't quite sure what they were getting." Then, there was "Market Mayhem: It's Out of Bernanke's Reach: There's little the Fed can do about the information gap behind investors' panic." Finally, there was this: "Regulators: More Paper Tiger Than Watchdog? The consumer product safety agency is overwhelmed and underfunded." Defective-product recalls were now an increasing economic drain, and the Consumer Product Safety Commission was less able to deal with the problem than ever before. "From a peak of nearly 1,000 [employees] in 1980 [prior to Reagan], CPSC's head count has fallen to 400."

Although the stock market rally on the day after President Bush's "re-"election was based upon sheer fantasy, there was good reason for the stocks of corrupt firms to rise that day. And those were the stocks that rose the most. Reuters then headlined, "Halliburton Surges After Bush Re-Election," and reported, "Shares in problem-plagued Halliburton Co. rose to their highest level in more than three years on Wednesday." But that's not actually good economic news; it's bad. When corrupt firms benefit, the majority of companies — which aren't corrupt — suffer. A stock market surge that makes more sense for corrupt firms than for honest ones is good for insiders, but it's bad for everyone else.

Shortly after Democrats won back control of Congress via the November 2006 elections, the *Wall Street Journal* bannered, on 21 March 2007, "Halliburton Signals Boom Is Fading: Profit Is to Fall Short," and reported that, "Halliburton ... disclosed that its first-quarter results would come in below expectations." Perhaps the reason wasn't the change in the Party controlling Congress; perhaps it was the reasons that Halliburton mentioned, such as its oil-field service business being exceptionally concentrated in U.S. wells, which were going down while foreign wells were going up. In other words, perhaps it was due to many years of simply abysmal corporate management, which relied upon corruption rather than upon production to generate the firm's profits. But

Halliburton's economic fate depended upon the Republican Party, just the same.

How often do we hear it said that the Republican Party is the world's biggest protection racket? Not at all — and yet that's precisely what it is. The amount of money pouring through it is immense, and it usually dwarfs what the Democratic Party is able to raise from their numerically much larger, but typically far less well-heeled, base.

And this money-advantage isn't the *only* advantage that the gangsters' Party has: the culture's predominant religious-based values also support the Republicans, whereas science-based values do not, as of yet in human history, have any institutional underpinning that's at all comparable to the churches and the clergy.

The myth that conservatives are better for a nation's economy than are progressives, is driven not by the masses but by the elite, the insiders who benefit from this deception. That's the aristocrats and the theocrats. And thus, despite all of the elite support which has been cited here for this myth, the *Wall Street Journal* bannered on 2 October 2007, "GOP Is Losing Grip On Core Business Vote," and Jackie Calmes reported that WSJ/NBC News polls since 1990 showed a steep fall-off in public support for the Republican over the Democratic Party on the question "Which party would do a better job at reducing the federal deficit?" The switch away from citing the Republican Party started right after the 1994 Newt Gingrich Congress, and by 2007, 42% favored the Democratic Party, and only 18% favored the Republican Party, on this question. Furthermore, the Democratic Party was now widely favored by the public on "Dealing with the economy," "Controlling government spending," and "Dealing with taxes." By this late a time in the G.W. Bush Administration, the only remaining people who still possessed faith in conservatives to run the economy were the elite themselves. Many of the mass suckers no longer had faith.

But, during the Religious Age, the elite still control, just as they did during the Tribal Age.

Consequently, progressive parties, such as America's Democrats, are institutionally bereft. This is the reason why dominant conservative parties, like America's Republicans, are generally politically more successful in our era than the dominant progressive parties. Lots of people have more faith in the gangsters than in progressive politicians. Faith in the "invisible hand" of God is reinforced every Sunday morning. Whereas the Bible asserts that a government should serve God, the U.S. Constitution asserts that the U.S. Government should serve the people — the ruled.

In no nation is democracy yet secure. The danger still exists that a conservative electorate will tolerate abolishing democracy, and will even support a fascist government. We live in an age of transition; it's a dangerous time.

Because of this solid institutional foundation of conservatism, many people who "ought to know better," such as the members of the CED, respect conservatism, even though their enemy is actually conservatism, and they just don't know it; they can't recognize that their own political Party, the Republicans, is controlled by elite gangsters. This doesn't make sense to them; they're confused. To such dupes, "conservatism" is associated with rectitude; not with a sophisticated kind of gangsterism.

These people might learn better if they were to read the 2003 *Saving Capitalism from the Capitalists*, by Raghuram Rajan and Luigi Zingales. Applying an international perspective that's too commonly lacking in such analyses, the authors conclude that the biggest enemies of capitalism are the aristocracy — insiders, "big business," the very same people who are generally believed to be the chief beneficiaries of capitalism (but who actually benefit from fascism instead). The authors (one of whom, Zingales, was also a co-author, that same year, of a major article studying the impact of religious beliefs on economic beliefs, "People's Opium? Religion and Economic Attitudes") present a sound nine-point program to increase capitalism and decrease fascism, and their proposals include increasing estate taxes, the social safety-net, and antitrust enforcement, as well as some other policies that the aristocracy constantly propagandize against.

Here's another, and associated, big myth: Conservatives are more moral than liberals. The reality here is that conservatives, being more religious, are more corrupt than liberals. (We've already documented this. As for the Zingales co-authored study of religion and economic beliefs, it found that religious people are more trusting, and also more bigoted, a combination which would support and even invite the depredations of the aristocracy. Their study also found that religious individuals are more intolerant of violating the law. In a democracy, where the Law is Man-made instead of from God, non-religious individuals tend to be more respecting of the democracy's laws, whereas religious believers are deluded to believe that morality comes instead from God's Law provided in Scripture. Thus, the kinds of corruption that conservatives tend especially to practice are probably generally shadings of the law, instead of outright violations of it. Such corruption can also include writing the laws so as to favor themselves and their friends.) And progressives, being not religious at all, are the least corrupt of all. Science is the way of honesty; religion is the way of lies. Without corruption, there's no call for faith — faith is then not needed, because science will provide support. Similarly, without honesty, there is no possibility of science — science isn't feasible with dishonesty, because the only support for dishonesty is faith. Without faith, dishonesty doesn't stand a chance. Without science, honesty doesn't stand a chance. The two epistemologies are exactly opposite in every way.

An age of transition is naturally difficult to figure out. It's made even more so by the constant propaganda emanating from the corrupters — churches, universities, etc. — who peddle the conservative line, be that pure conservative, or the diluted liberal type.

Throughout this perilous period, conservatives fraudulently refer to their criminogenic politics as the politics of economic freedom and of moral responsibility. They, of

course, ignore the freedom — economic and otherwise — of
their numerous victims, and they ignore accountability
entirely. (They believe in responsibility, the public's
obligations to those in power; but they ignore accountability,
the obligations that the powerful have to the public.)

Here's a good example of how they do this: Myron
Magnet was the editor of the magazine of the extremely
conservative Manhattan Institute, which itself was financed
primarily by still other far-right-wing foundations and
aristocrats: primarily by the Lynde and Harry Bradley
Foundation, Richard Mellon Scaife, the J.M. Olin Foundation,
and the Smith Richardson Foundation. On 20 July 2004, Dr.
Magnet headlined an op-ed in the American aristocrats'
leading newspaper, the *Wall Street Journal,* "Freedom vs.
Dependency," and in it he attributed poverty to the personal
laziness of the poor, and to liberals' tolerance of the laziness of
the poor. He criticized those who say that there is any
problem with the economic or political "system" in America,
and asserted, to the contrary, "Blame instead the enormous
changes unfolding in American culture in exactly those years:
the sexual revolution, the counterculture's contempt for the
'system,' the celebration of drugs, dropping out, and
rebellion." In other words: blame the presumably middle class
liberals for the poverty of the poor, the lower class. A man like
this, with such stereotypical right-wing thinking, receives
huge funding from aristocrats, because his garbage tells them
what they want to hear — that they're just great. He exploits,
in the general American public (infected as it is with so many
religious biases) the negative stereotype of liberals, as being
people who find no problem with irresponsibility, neither
with that of the middle class, nor with that of poor people. On
this shoddy intellectual basis, this leading think-tank scholar
blamed not just the poor for their being irresponsible, but also
the liberal non-poor, for their supposedly encouraging the
irresponsibility of the poor. While some liberals (especially
religious liberals) do, indeed, think in the stereotyped way
that such a stereotypic reactionary thinker attacks, this is not

necessarily to say that the American "system" is terrific, as Magnet and other conservatives simply assume to be the case. A religious society cannot be let off a scientist's analytical hook quite so easily. The biggest hoax behind such stereotypical conservative thinking is that it ignores the massive extent to which the problem, in a religious culture, such as in America, isn't irresponsibility, so much as it is *unaccountability* — which conservatives prefer to ignore altogether.

To the extent that conservatives do pay attention to accountability, they strongly oppose it. This is demonstrated not only by their opposition to the tort system, but also by their opposition to the only other governmental system that has been established to deal with the crimes of corporations and the rich, which is the regulatory system. Republicans are famously critical of regulation by governmental agencies. So, Republicans don't actually want *either* of the two systems that have been established to provide accountability for the crimes of the aristocracy — neither torts, nor regulation. Republicans wish aristocrats to be able to rob and otherwise exploit serfs, and to have no accountability at all — not even the tepid forms that have been established by our Religious society.

It's worth noting that these conservatives oppose all accountability. They aren't saying that upper-class crimes should be addressed by criminal laws, and should be held accountable the same way that the crimes committed by poor people are held responsible: to criminal fines, imprisonment of the individual perpetrators, and restitution to the individual victims. That would be the progressive proposal; conservatives would oppose it ferociously.

Instead, conservatives aim to destroy even the all-too-weak systems that currently exist for providing accountability to the crimes privileged crooks perpetrate.

Big-corporate executives, who are the strongest source of the Republican Party's funding, don't even want to be held accountable by their stockholders. For example, on 5 September 2007, the *Wall Street Journal* bannered "Scholars

Link Success of Firms To Lives of CEOs," and Mark
Maremont reported on "an emerging — and controversial —
area of financial research that delves into the lives and
personalities of executives in search of links to stock prices
and corporate performance." One of the striking findings was
that within three years of an executive's moving into a
mansion larger than 10,000 square feet, his company's stock
price underperformed the market by 20%. By contrast, within
three years of an executive's moving into a residence smaller
than that, his company's stock price outperformed the market
by 20%. This "Edifice Complex" suggested that accountability
for job-performance did not exist at all, or else was in the exact
opposite direction from what supporters of the "invisible
hand" of God presume.

By the summer of 2004, the Bush Administration was
even pushing total war against accountability. On July 25th,
The New York Times headlined, "In a Shift, Bush Moves to
Block Medical Suits," and opened: "The Bush administration
has been going to court to block lawsuits by consumers who
say they have been injured by prescription drugs and medical
devices. The administration contends that consumers cannot
recover damages for such injuries if the products have been
approved by the Food and Drug Administration. In court
papers, the Justice Department acknowledges that this
position reflects 'a change in governmental policy.'" The Bush
Administration was arguing that the two separate systems
that have been established to deal with accountability cannot
apply simultaneously: only one or the other can apply; only
torts or else regulation.

This is like saying that a murderer cannot be tried for a
federal crime if he's being tried also for violating a state law
regarding that same alleged incident. However, that is not the
way the ban against double jeopardy had been interpreted or
applied in the past. And the Bush Administration never
attempted to apply such an interpretation except in this one
way — i.e., *to protect aristocrats.*

The Bush Administration was, in effect, arguing that if a governmental regulatory agency okays a particular product or practice, even if by means of governmental corruption (which Republicans constantly promote), then there cannot be any liability whatsoever attaching to that product or practice: any damages that it might happen to cause will be entirely uncompensated; there will be no accountability whatsoever, neither for negligence, nor for fraud, nor for any other reason.

This is the authoritarian dream: "Trust us." It's total faith. The chicken must not question the fox who is in charge of the chicken coop. There would be no opportunity for any sort of appeals. And, if corruption occurs, or if there's a mistake due to negligence, or even if there is fraud — and all of these things happen routinely in any conservative society — then the victim will bear the resulting losses 100%, regardless whether he's totally innocent, and even if a government official colluded with executives of the regulated firm in order to win approval of his dangerous product. The perpetrating business will have no liability, because the governmental regulatory authority had approved of its product — even if that approval was itself corrupt.

Furthermore, the Bush Administration was doing everything it possibly could to vitiate or weaken all of the regulatory agencies, so as to assure that the American public would be protected by nothing at all. On 14 August 2004, *The New York Times* headlined "Out of Spotlight, Bush Overhauls U.S. Regulations." The reporter, Joel Brinkley, said that the Bush Administration was systematically gutting federal regulations by rule-making buried "deep within the turgid pages of the Federal Register," outside of congressional oversight, and away from the prying eyes of the hordes of journalists. One of many examples he cited was a ruling on April 21st, "that would forbid the public release of some data relating to unsafe motor vehicles." Brinkley said the reason given for the rule-change was that "publicizing the information would cause 'substantial competitive harm' to manufacturers." In other words, were this data to be published, manufacturers of dangerous cars would suffer in competition against manufacturers of safe cars. The Bush Administration, which did everything it could to assist rather than to prosecute white-collar criminality (such as the manufacture of needlessly dangerous automobiles that kill and maim unnecessarily many innocent victims), was thus ruling that there mustn't be competitive advantage to be gained by manufacturing safer cars. Brinkley continued, "'My thoughts go back to Herbert Hoover,' said Robert Dallek, the presidential historian. 'No president could have been more friendly to business than Hoover' until the Bush administration." Of course, history furthermore records that that *kind* of "more friendly to business" attitude actually created the Great Depression, which wasn't *really* "friendly to business," regardless of what some historians might suggest.

On 3 December 2007, *USA Today* bannered "Report: FDA So Underfunded, Consumers Are Put at Risk," and Julie Schmit reported that, "The Food and Drug Administration is so underfunded and understaffed that it's putting U.S. consumers at risk in terms of food and drug safety, an advisory panel to the FDA says in a report." The report "details a 'plethora of inadequacies' in the agency, including ... inadequate inspections, ... a depleted FDA staff, ... a 'badly broken' food-import system and food supply 'that grows riskier each year, ... a workforce with a 'dearth' of scientists," and "an 'obsolete' information-technology system." A member of the panel said, "These people were horrified by what they found." The report was titled "FDA Science and Mission at Risk."

It stated:

"Science at the FDA is in a precarious position. ... The impact of the deficiency is profound precisely because science is at the heart of everything FDA does. The Agency will flounder and ultimately fail without a strong scientific foundation. ...

"The Subcommittee found substantial weaknesses across the Agency. ... The nation's food supply is at risk. ... Due to constrained resources and lack of adequate staff, FDA is engaged in reactive regulatory priority setting or a fire-fighting regulatory posture. ...

"The turnover rate in FDA science staff in key scientific areas is twice that of other government agencies. ... FDA's failure to retain and motivate its workforce puts FDA's mission at risk. ...

"The Subcommittee was extremely disturbed at the state of the FDA IT [information technology] infrastructure. ... Systems fail frequently, and even email systems are unstable. ... Recent system failures have resulted in loss of FDA data. ... There is no backup of these records. ...

"[Consequences are] an import system that is badly broken, a food supply that grows riskier each year, and an information infrastructure that was identified as a source of risk in every Center and program. ... We conclude that FDA can no longer fulfill its mission. ...

"Crises are now realities and American lives are at risk. ...

"In his recent Executive Order announcing an Inter-Agency Working Group on Import Safety, President Bush stated that the current system must be fixed 'within available resources.' We can state unequivocally that the system cannot be fixed 'within available resources.' ... The current resources have clearly been insufficient to support the regulatory science and regulatory services of the FDA.

"The demands on the FDA have soared due to the extraordinary advance of swcientific discoveries. ... The resources [at FDA] have not increased in proportion to the demands."

Perhaps George W. Bush and the Republican voters and financial backers who placed him into power would say that Bush was correct, and that this study (and others it cited which had been done earlier by the National Academies of Science, and by others), had it wrong, and that solutions could be established "within available resources." Bush had already been President for seven years, and he had had Republican controlled congresses for most of that time. The only conclusion, if he was right on that, was that his administration of the FDA had been purely a disaster of wasted resources, not also a disaster of underfunding regulatory functions. Either way, Republicans were 100% accountable for the problems that this report observed, and Bush couldn't lie his way out of guilt for this disaster.

Placing foxes in charge of the hen house doesn't produce a thriving hen house; it produces victors eating victims, and that's not an economy — it's just war by the powerful against the weak. Corrupt companies benefited from Republicans' squelching of accountability, but everyone else suffered from it.

Here's a question: Which U.S. President since 1900 entered, or was re-elected to, office with the highest public expectations that his policies would produce a thriving U.S. economy? According to a chart published on the front page of the business section of *The New York Times* on New Year's Day of 2005, under an article headlined "Late Stock Market Rally Makes 2004 a Winning Year," in which was shown the "Change in the Dow, day before the presidential election to end of the year," the biggest gain in the Dow Jones Industrial average for any incoming or re-elected President in over a century was for Herbert Hoover, elected in 1928: from the time of his election until the end of that year, the Dow soared 16.5%. The Crash occurred less than a year after he was elected, and his policies dealing with it were disastrous and helped turn it into The Great Depression. Not only is the old conservative adage "Fifty million Frenchmen can't be wrong" wrong, but 200 million Americans can also be wrong, and so can the public anywhere be wrong, because every culture is a stacked deck during the Religious Age — stacked high with prejudices, which are often wrong. In fact, of the seventeen Presidents whom the stock market welcomed with immediate gains, eleven were Republicans, whereas of the ten who were greeted with immediate losses, only five were Republicans. A long-term investor cannot do better than to enter the stock market during the first two years after a Republican president has been replaced by a Democrat, and to leave the stock market during the first two years after a Democratic president has been replaced by a Republican: the stock market overvalues Republicans and undervalues Democrats, because most investors during the Religious Age invest on the basis of faith, not on the basis of science.

Naturally, therefore, on the day after Democrats retook control of Congress following 12 years in the wilderness, Reuters headlined, 8 November 2006, "Stocks Seen Down After Democratic Poll Upset," and reported that, "U.S. Stock futures pointed to a sharply lower start on Wall Street on Wednesday after Democrats swept Republicans from power." Stocks, most of which are held by the wealthiest 5% of the nation's population, and not by the poorer 95%, were held predominantly by people of astoundingly low intelligence — people who were so duped by the top 1%, the insiders, that most stockholders actually believed the myth that stocks perform better under Republican than under Democratic rule.

A different expression of the Religious worship of power is the common misperception that large corporations are more efficient or better for investors than are medium-sized or small firms. This falsehood, too, is especially promulgated by conservative aristocrats and their media, such as the opinion pages of the *Wall Street Journal*. For example, Alan Murray opined there, on 15 June 2005, under the heading (itself typical of their prejudices) "Backlash Against CEOs Could Go Too Far," that, "Despite their now-all-too-obvious flaws, large corporations have been the great wealth generators of the past half century." That's simply *false*, yet he didn't think that it even needed to be documented — so readily do most of his authoritarian newspaper's readers *agree* with this prejudice. And he provided no documentation, because there wasn't any. The actual fact was, instead, that small-cap companies have, with a remarkable degree of consistency, delivered higher average rates of return to investors than mid-caps, and that the lowest returns of all have gone to investors in large-cap stocks. This applied during "the past half century," just as it had for the half-century before. So, the *exact opposite* of Murray's statement was true.

In a society where faith is respected, and dominates, there's no penalty for peddling falsehoods; so, power reigns, and the falsehoods which power favors are widely believed to be true.

The reason why Democrats are immensely better at producing a thriving economy than are Republicans, is that progressives recognize what conservatives do not: an economy can be no more successful than it is accountable. A conservative cannot accept this, because a conservative is opposed to accountability, when he even recognizes the existence of accountability. Thus, feudal economies are never thriving economies.

The conservative aristocrats have hornswoggled the masses of fools everywhere to believe that the less accountable that aristocrats are, the better it will be for those fools, and they've defined this lack of accountability as "freedom" and as "liberty," which is, in fact, true only for aristocrats, while unaccountability actually *reduces* the freedom and liberty of everyone else.

These aristocrats are very good at deflecting blame, and clergy sell the ideology that facilitates this: credit goes upward to God, while blame goes downward to the public — to democracy. On 10 September 2007, the lead editorial in the *Wall Street Journal* headlined "Congress and Recession" and blamed the new recession on Congress's having been (though just barely) under Democratic majority control for the prior seven months, since late January 2007. "Add the promise of every Democratic Presidential candidate to repeal the Bush tax cuts [on aristocrats] if he or she wins in 2008, and no wonder investors are growing more cautious," said the aristocracy The Republican Fed wasn't to blame for the coming recession. The Republican President wasn't to blame for it. The collapse of the housing bubble that those Republicans had built up wasn't to blame for it. A second editorial was headlined "Class in New Jersey" and it celebrated the defeat in New Jersey of a class action lawsuit against Merck for Vioxx. The third editorial, "Licensed to Kill," blamed licensing regulation as harming the economy, but granted that, "The government's role in protecting the public from fraud may argue in favor of licensing in some very specialized, learned professions." Nothing was said there about the government's *obligation* to protect the public from fraud. It was just a "role," perhaps "the government's interest," but *not* "the government's obligation" to protect the public from fraudsters — such as themselves. Whatever could be done to *diminish* accountability received the *support* of the owners, editors, and managers, of the aristocratic Wall Street Journal.

The two major political mechanisms for the accountability of aristocrats have been government regulatory agencies, and the tort system of civil legal liability (such as class-actions); and aristocrats have demonized both as constituting major impediments to the economy — though these mechanisms for accountability have actually been fundamental to the dynamic growth of the American economy. On 15 April 2006, the *Wall Street Journal* headlined "The Weekend Interview with Hank Greenberg / By Kimberly A. Strassel," who was identified as "a member of the Journal's editorial board." This op-ed was yet another shot in the *WSJ*'s war against the prominent white-collar-crime-buster, New York Attorney General (AG) Eliot Spitzer, who had forced Mr. Greenberg out of the insurance giant, A.I.G. The article's title and main point was "You Couldn't Build an A.I.G. Today" because of regulators such as Mr. Spitzer; the sub-head was "An insurance titan expounds on the dimming of America" that was also being attributed here to the policies of the Democratic Party. Ms. Strassel's tone toward her subject was worshipful. She wrote: "Mr. Greenberg hasn't dimmed, but he believes America has. 'You couldn't build an A.I.G.

today,' he explains. Overbearing regulators, new corporate
governance rules, protectionism, a failing tort system,
prosecutors unleashed — these, as he sees them, are the
obstacles to corporate greatness. And Mr. Greenberg is
uniquely positioned to know. ... At this time last year, he was
running the world's largest business insurer. Then along came
Mr. Spitzer, on the prowl for another headline-generating
takedown." Ms. Strassel referred contemptuously to "the AG's
... suspect tactics" in that "takedown," though she failed to
provide any details of them — the faithful could accept such a
slur without documentation. Her article's thrust was that
people like Greenberg were the champions of capitalism,
whereas people like Spitzer were the demons responsible for
"the dimming of America." In a religious country, this black-
is-white, white-is-black, viewpoint has always been essential
to the gospel of the "invisible hand" of God, and has
"explained" to the faithful how the economy works, and how
it *ought* to work. But at the very same time as the aristocrats'
newspaper published this trash, *BusinessWeek* headlined
"Flight of the Investor Class: Defections are endangering the
GOP's hold on power." Ironically, what had been driving
down small investors' previous (as of 2004) 61% support of
the Republican over the Democratic Party, to only 42% now,
wasn't so much the miserable economic record of Republicans
— not even their miserable current record under Bush — but
was instead the Bush Administration's catastrophically bad
response to Hurricane Katrina. "Pollster John Zogby says the
President's decline [among small investors] started with the
bungled reaction to Katrina." Nonetheless, "Bruce Bagley, 53,
a small-business owner in Santa Rosa, Calif., is more afraid of
what would happen if Democrats take Congress. Investors
would have 'a bull's-eye on [their] back,' he claims." The
Republican executives who perpetrate fraud against their
investors wouldn't have a bulls-eye on their backs — those
fraudsters' *victims* would. Black is white, and white is black,
and faith is the way to know this. It seems that, even when the
faithful reduced their allegiance to the Republican Party, they

retained their faith; and this faith kept many boobs within the Republican fold. Their faith blinded them from understanding what was happening and why. Conservative aristocrats know quite well that such fools are essential to their own success — not only in politics, but also in business. These aristocrats live off such victims.

Alexandra Spieldoch didn't share Strassel's faith. Spieldoch's July 2002 essay on the internet, "When a Terrible Situation Gets Worse: Reflections on Argentina," explained how the Argentine economic collapse in 2001 had resulted from a total lack of accountability, including especially a lack of accountability for Citibank, and for other institutions of the international aristocracy. She noted that, "As a conditionality for bailout of Argentina, the IMF recently recommended that the Argentine Senate overturn a 1974 ['Economic Subversion'] law that allowed bankers, business owners and government officials to be prosecuted for financial crimes. The law would also have enabled federal courts to investigate the capital flight in 2001. Unfortunately, it was overturned [on 30 May 2002]." The IMF demanded that the Argentine Government not prosecute the insiders who had gamed the nation's economic catastrophe, so that only the masses of economic outsiders would be left holding the empty looted bag at the end. This was how "the invisible hand" of God was supposed to function; and, in the end, it did function that way, and there was no accountability when the Argentine economy collapsed. However, this isn't the way of successful economies. Spieldoch wrote of "The Cultural Tolerance for National Corruption," which had prevailed in Argentina ever since Juan Peron's fascist reign started in 1943, and which the nation's culture never renounced afterwards. The IMF was now taking essentially the same position as Argentina's fascists had, only representing a different nation's aristocracy. This was might-makes-right politics. Spieldoch implicitly recognized the falsity of such views as the Law and Economics movement from the Chicago school of economics, which says that laws should be based upon economic theory, instead of economic theory being based upon the society's realities, which include the laws. Her critique was directed against what she called this "neo-liberal" view. However, religion was actually more basic to such might-makes-right attitudes than were any such merely academic rationalizations.

What chiefly keeps conservatism (Religious-Age morality) going, is the myth that some supernatural heaven can be won in an afterlife if only a person pleases The Almighty above. Morally, everything therefore gets translated into responsibility — *to The Lord*. Thus, accountability doesn't exist. Everything is based solely upon *trust in God*.

Aristocrats tend to believe that they're God's People because: Otherwise, why would they *be* aristocrats? If they were born richer than everybody else, or (as they often like to think) smarter than everybody else or simply better than everybody else, then it's not because they *did* that, so it must have been the *will of The Almighty*. This is the "invisible hand" of God at work, nobody else could have done it. On 19 June 2009, Megan McArdle posted at business.theatlantic.com, "Fear of Failure," a discussion of the commencement address that the aristocrat Paul Tudor Jones II (worth an estimated $3.3 billion in the March 2007 *Forbes*) had given nine days earlier at the elite Buckley School. (The title of his address was "Perfect Failure," meaning that failure is merely the way a person perfects himself.) McArdle aptly noted: "This seems like a pretty safe bet when you're talking to Buckley students, who have an ample safety net underneath them to allow them to bounce back from nearly any failure. But would he really say this to, say, a 55 year old man who'd just been fired from his sales job? Bad things — persistent bad things — happen to good people, and while it's comforting to think of them as merely a waystation, for lots of people that isn't really true." In fact, aristocrats often thrive the most when their employees are the *most* desperate, because then the employees will be more compliant and work even harder out of a greater fear of being fired, and so they'll be more "productive." And they'll accept lower pay. So, was Mr. Tudor Jones (whose cousin owned one of the world's largest cotton-marketing companies and had set him up with commodites broker Eli Tullis, who taught him the skills he used a few years later to start Tudor Investment Corp.) going to be worried that *non*-aristocrats were having their government safety nets pulled out from under them by Republicans? On the other hand, their employees and other non-aristocrats wouldn't *vote* for Republican governments unless those peons believed in the "invisible hand" of God. So, aristocrats *needed* the theocrats and other peddlers of faith.

It's all driven ultimately by greed on the part of aristocrats, and fear of death on the part of everyone else. At the base of the pyramid of exploitation is religion, which needs its money from the aristocrats, and its volunteers from the believers. Conservatism is *death-obsessed*. Furthermore, people who tend to vote Republican are driven also by religious fears *for their children* (such as that they will become homosexual) — even though the Republican Party has historically left the subsequent generation diminished stock and other investment values, as well as diminished retirements, healthcare security, etc., and has consequently enhanced dangers instead of enhanced safety, both for parents and for their children. So, not only is conservatism death-obsessed, but it provides an "inerrant Scripture" containing a mythology that "rationalizes" its life-destroying travesties (including bigotries, "social issues," and false "values").

People don't tend to notice these complex realities; and, besides, religion has inculcated the very simple (but false) idea that safety results from people's pleasing The Almighty. The way to please The Almighty is described in Scripture, which was written to serve the needs of the elite in its own time. The obedient, submissive, compliant, conformist person makes the ideal slave or serf; and the objective of religion is therefore to mold the public in this way. However, that's not the way of the thriving, dynamic, economy and society, towards which human culture is evolving. It's instead the way of the

aristocratic/theocratic society, and the mass poverty, we try to
leave behind.

To continue from the last example cited, automobile
fatalities have long been the leading cause of deaths in the
United States, and certainly a thriving and successful
American economy becomes more so whenever auto fatalities
go down. This increase in car-safety has actually been
happening, because of Democrats, and it has required
government enforcing accountability upon manufacturers
every step of the way in order to make it happen. Figures
from the National Highway Traffic Administration show that
between 1966 and 2003, the number of motor vehicle deaths
per 100 million vehicle miles driven in the United States
plunged 75%, down to an amazing *only one fourth* of the death-
rate of "the good old days" in 1966. This resulted from things
like government mandated crash-tests, requirements for
manufacturers to equip cars with seat belts, etc. — all being
regulatory demands that Democrats pushed relentlessly, and
that auto industry executives and their Republican Party and
other fake "libertarian" supporters fought tooth and nail, as
"violating the free market," and as threatening to depress the
American economy, instead of to *improve* it, as it has since
demonstrably and overwhelmingly done. These mandates
didn't even hurt the automakers themselves, and produced a
competitive advantage to the ones who excelled on safety
features. Yet the True Believers in "the invisible hand" of God
controlling things, rather than in Man doing so via democratic
government, persist in the myth that their aristocratic "free
market" — which maximizes freedom *only* for the aristocracy,
at everyone else's expense — ends up miraculously producing
a booming economy. Conservatives, supporters of that false
aristocratic line, who vote for Republicans, are motivated
actually by their fear of death, but, being the fools that they
are, they're nonetheless electing Republican politicians, who
are consistently fighting *against* the very things that have
caused automobiles to become four times safer in less than 40
years. On 10 August 2006, Matthew L. Wald headlined in *The*

New York Times, "Study Credits Vehicles, but Not Drivers, for Better Road Safety," and reported: "The death rate per million miles traveled has fallen almost every year since 1966, although it was up slightly in 2005, according to a preliminary estimate by the government's National Highway Traffic Safety Administration. It would have risen in the 10 years ended 2004, rather than falling 16.8 percent, if not for the improvements in vehicles," according to a study by the Insurance Institute for Highway Safety. "In fact, without design changes that have made vehicles safer, including the growing prevalence of air bags, the death toll on the nation's roads would be higher by about 5,000 people annually, more than 11 percent of last year's total." Conservative serfs vote for their aristocratic masters, who then abuse them — and all outsiders — without mercy. The belief in conservatism (even if by its euphemism "libertarianism") is based solely upon religious myths. Behind these myths are elite gangsters. That's the reason why Democrats have historically been overwhelmingly demonstrated to boost the American economy, while Republicans have been overwhelmingly proven to produce economic failure for the nation.

The biggest enemies of the automotive industry in the United States were not liberals, or Democrats, in Washington or elsewhere, who sought legislation to increase automotive safety, or fuel economy; the greatest enemies of this auto industry were the automotive executives who (often supported by labor leaders) opposed those things. Thus, Japanese and other auto companies produced more-fuel-efficient cars, which were economically more competitive in most countries, and ultimately even in the U.S. itself. If America's car companies had supported instead of opposed Democratic policy initiatives on these things (and also on socializing health insurance, which would have removed that huge cost from America's car-makers), then the U.S. automakers would have become vastly more competitive, not only in the U.S., but internationally.

On 3 September 2007, *BusinessWeek* bannered "The Big Problem With Big Fish: Feeble inspections make it easy for importers to slip through high-mercury seafood." John Carey described the scam: "To get fish cleared by the FDA, ... importers simply have to show that five samples of fish are under the limit. The importer gets to pick the lab to do that analysis. It can also choose the actual fish for testing. That enables importers to game the system, argue the FDA's own scientists." Conservatives are against regulation. In their "free market," regulation wouldn't exist, or else would be purely voluntary and so have no force of law behind it. But the results were inevitably millions of people getting mercury poisoning, which was a pure expense for the nation's economy, not only for the poisoned individuals but also for their employers (days lost from work, etc.). "The Boston-based restaurant chain Legal Sea Foods is one business that has sought to allay concerns by doing its own testing." It's hardly the efficient way to protect the public, but faith in the "invisible hand" of God reigns during the Religious Age. The very following week, on September 10th, the same magazine bannered "Fear and Loathing at the Airport," and opened, "When Marion C. Blakey took over at the Federal Aviation Administration in 2002, she was determined to fix an air travel system battered by terrorism," but, "Five years later, ... it's clear she failed. Almost everything about flying is worse than when she arrived. Greater are the risks, the passenger headaches, and the costs in lost productivity."

In a democracy, the people who hate (democratic) government are the aristocrats and the theocrats, and when they control the government the result might be good for themselves but it's hell on Earth for everyone else, and this *isn't* a good economy.

This conservative myth takes innumerable forms. For example, on 30 March 2006, John Kasich, who had been a loyal partisan Republican in Congress for 18 years, from Ohio, headlined an op-ed in the *Wall Street Journal*, "Buckeye GOP Circles the Drain," and he argued that "corruption has reigned" in the Ohio Republican Party, as "a direct result of one-party domination of the political process" there, which he blamed upon "Democratic incompetence" in Ohio. He was now an investment banker, and he was saying that the corruption "that is drowning the Ohio Republican Party" was caused by the state's Democrats. Kasich, whom the *WSJ* identified only as "a former Ohio congressman," was simultaneously being identified at Fox "News" as the host of "The Heartland with John Kasich," and as a "managing director at Lehman Brothers [which went bankrupt in 2008]." If Kasich didn't know better than to blame the pervasive Republican corruption upon Democrats, then only fools would have been investing with him. However, if he was instead lying in saying this, then only fools would have been investing with him. So, then: what's the difference? Either way, Kasich had to be a man of faith. And, either way, only people of faith would believe what he was saying. He was part of the problem, not part of its solution. He always had been.

Jared Diamond, in an op-ed in *The New York Times* on New Year's Day 2005, headlined "The Ends of the World as We Know Them," and he summarized the key points of his then-upcoming book, *Collapse: How Societies Choose or Fail to Succeed*. He boiled it down as follows: "A society contains a built-in blueprint for failure if the elite insulates itself from the consequences of its actions. That's why Maya kings, Norse Greenlanders and Easter Island chiefs made choices [insulating themselves from the consequences of their actions] that eventually undermined their societies. They themselves did not begin to feel deprived until they had irreversibly destroyed their landscape." As with his earlier *Guns, Germs and Steel*, he kept "safely" to examples from primitive societies. However, the bearing upon today's realities was now remarkably direct. Thus, one can reasonably conclude that the frosted glass on the limousines of the super-rich, and the gated communities in which many of these elites live, and all of the mechanisms that the conservatives have so carefully put in place to eliminate accountability, foretell a society's decline. It's only natural that Republicans are bad for the economy. The phenomenon that's been documented by Vinzant and others, concerning the United States, is fully in accord with Diamond's findings, which go all the way back to ancient times.

At the time of America's Iraq-invasion and for a long period afterward, Riverbend.blogspot.com was the leading blog by an Iraqi, reporting on the invasion/occupation from the standpoint of the invaded/occupied. On 26 April 2007, the blog's author finally announced that she and her family were about to join the millions who had already escaped from Iraq. America's invasion/occupation had created such hell for them, that losing everything they had was worth the escape from the civil war which George W. Bush and his fellow conservatives had caused them. She started by condemning the high wall that America was constructing to supposedly protect a Sunni neighborhood in Baghdad: "The wall, of course, will protect no one" she said — and it didn't. She answered those who replied, "It will be difficult for people to get into their special area to hurt them," by "It will also be difficult to get out." She compared what the Americans and Iraqi puppet government were doing with what the Nazis did to construct the "protective" wall around Warsaw's Jewish quarter. With thinly veiled condemnation of the religious fanatics in both America and Iraq, she said:

"The Wall is the latest effort to further break Iraqi society apart. Promoting and supporting civil war isn't enough, apparently — Iraqis have generally proven to be more tenacious and tolerant than their mullahs, ayatollahs, and Vichy leaders. It's time for America to physically divide and conquer — like Berlin before the wall came down or Palestine today. This way, they can continue chasing Sunnis out of 'Shia areas' and Shia out of 'Sunni areas'.

"I always hear the Iraqi pro-war crowd interviewed on television from foreign capitals (they can only appear on television from the safety of foreign capitals because I defy anyone to be publicly pro-war in Iraq). They refuse to believe that their religiously inclined, sectarian political parties fueled this whole Sunni/Shia conflict. They refuse to acknowledge that this situation is a direct result of the war and occupation. They go on and on about Iraq's history and how Sunnis and Shia were always in conflict and I hate that. I hate that a handful of expats who haven't been to the country in decades pretend to know more about it than people actually living there.

"I remember Baghdad before the war — one could live anywhere. We didn't know what our neighbors were — we didn't care. No one asked about religion or sect. No one bothered with what was considered a trivial topic: are you Sunni or Shia?"

The American contractors who were pumping millions into Republican Party coffers profited enormously from this invasion/occupation, but it split the entire world apart.

Conservatives were a disaster to every nation's economy both within and without.

The more progressive a society/culture/economy is, the more it will boom and grow. The more conservative, the more it will stagnate and decline. Michael J. Mandel, in a book review, "Seeing the Light of Growth," in the 26 December 2005 *BusinessWeek,* observed that, while Republicans talk constantly about economic growth, "Democrats seem to prefer to talk about economic security and redistribution." Isn't that observation odd? The Republican Party was, in fact, the party of redistribution, but from the poor to the rich, and that's why 25 years of Republican dominance in America, extending from about 1980 to 2005, caused the U.S. to plunge from having had the best wealth-distribution in the world, to having the worst wealth-distribution of any developed nation.

And the Republican Party was also the party of economic security, but *only* for those who already possessed the most economic security — the aristocracy. Meanwhile, the Democratic Party has been, for at least a century, the party of economic growth, because it has represented the interests of the nation, not of *merely* the aristocracy.

On 18 August 2006, Paul Krugman headlined in *The New York Times,* "Wages, Wealth And Politics," and he said: "I've been studying the long-term history of inequality in the United States. And it's hard to avoid the sense that it matters a lot which political party, or more accurately, which political

ideology rules Washington. Since the 1920's there have been
four eras" with very different rates of either shared or
unshared economic growth, and consistently when Democrats
have been federally dominant, economic growth has been
widely shared, whereas under Republican rule the wealth has
gone to only the very wealthiest.

A party of economic stagnation will favor abolishing
estate taxes, and will do little or nothing to reduce the taxes on
labor-derived income. A party of economic growth will
exhibit the exact reverse orientation. But the stagnant-
economy party will enjoy the reputation of fostering economic
growth, and the booming-economy party will suffer the
reputation of fostering economic stagnation. That's religion.
That's faith. And that's the way America has been been
increasingly headed ever since the aristocracy and the
conservative clergy joined forces following the Civil Rights
Act of 1964, to transform the U.S. into a fascist nation. The
takeover of the White House in 1980 was especially key. Since
that time, not only had economic equality been replaced by
economic inequality, but taxes on estates have been replaced
by taxes on personal incomes. According to estimates by the
Office of Management and Budget in 2006, Federal
Government income that year derived 44.3% from individual
income taxes, and 34.7% from Social Security "payroll" taxes:
fully 79% of federal income derived from individual income
taxes. Only 13.8% derived from corporate income taxes, and
7.2% derived from everything else. A quarter-century of
predominantly Republican rule had left the Federal
Government almost entirely dependent upon taxes of
individuals' labor, and almost not at all dependent upon taxes
of estates and other aristocratic gifts and bequests. Moreover,
complex tax rules provided top-income earners with
loopholes that regular wage earners could only dream of.

President Bush continued his class-war even after
Democrats won Congress in the November 2006 elections. For
example, on 11 April 2007, the *Wall Street Journal* bannered
"Deferred-Pay Rules a Win for Executives," and Theo Francis

reported that, "Nearly four years in the making, ... the Treasury Department has released its deferred-compensation regulations," and, "the new rules will let hundreds of thousands of executives who defer their compensation continue to enjoy big tax breaks without facing additional restrictions beyond those in place in recent years." This Treasury rulemaking was, in effect, a huge tax cut for top executives.

At the time of the American Civil War, Abraham Lincoln's Republican Party was created as a restoration of the populist values which Thomas Jefferson had embodied, and which Jefferson's Democratic party had, after Jefferson's time, compromised and eventually lost. Lincoln's own hero was Jefferson. They both stood opposed to the plantation owners who supported slavery — their era's aristocracy. Today's version of that aristocracy are the big-corporate Republican executives, who now farm the government.

Numerous news stories have been published decrying the soaring incomes to executives during this era when incomes to everyone else have been stagnating. The prevailing view has been that executives were becoming unpopular. But this widespread view was false. In fact, a Fox News/Opinion Dynamics poll taken on "February 7-8, 2006" and published on "9 February 06," included the question: "Which one of the following would you rather see as our next president?" The highest percentage of respondents, 33%, chose "a business leader." Tied in second place were "a military general" (another authoritarian icon), and "a career politician," both at 21%. No other option scored higher than mere single digits. The most popular choice, "a business leader," reflected the widespread view that this heavily Republican category were the people selected by "the invisible hand" of God. More realistic would have been to think of them as the top gangsters. And when the Party that those gangsters support has been in power in the U.S., this nation's economy has turned in its very worst performances.

And yet, such economic performance has benefited those extremely wealthy gangsters. For example, the Bush Administration claimed that Bush's tax cuts on capital gains and dividends benefited all Americans. But look at two visuals from a 30 January 2006 study by the Center on Budget and Policy Priorities, "Capital Gains and Dividend Tax Cuts: Data Make Clear that High-Income Households Benefit the Most":

"FIGURE 1" was "Capital Gains and Dividend Income Is Larger Share of Total Income of High-Income Households, 2003," and it showed that for people making $0-50,000, it was about 1%; for people making %50,000-$100,000, it was about 2%; for people making $100,000-$200,000, it was about 3%; for people making $200,000-$1,000,000, it was about 11%; and for people making $1,000,000+, it was about 32%. Thus: the especially low cap-gains and dividend tax-rates of 15%, which were less than half of the normal 35% income-tax rate for incomes of more than $1,000,000, were of significant benefit almost *only to the super-rich*. This enormous gift from the Republican Party was well compensated to Republican politicians' political campaigns, because $1,000,000+ "earners" (if one should even *call* cap-gains and dividends "*earned*" income) were the people who chiefly funded politicians' campaigns for election and re-election. George W. Bush and congressional Republicans passed into law this special low 15% rate of taxation for this actually unearned income. The very wealthy gangsters who had no conscience to worry about benefits to the broader population were naturally viewing Bush's economic policies as being terrific. But only a fool would think that those policies were good for *most* Americans. Instead: this was simply a massive shifting of the taxation-burden downward, from the aristocrats, onto the public.

"FIGURE 2" was "Extension of Capital Gains and Dividend Tax Cut Primarily Benefits High-Income Households, 2009," and it showed that this extension (which the Republicans in 2010 demanded from Obama and the

Democrats in order for the Federal Government to avoid defaulting for the first time in U.S. history), benefited earners of $0-$50,000, $11 per year; $50,000-$100,000, $77 per year; $100,000-$200,000, $228 per year; $200,000-$1,000,000, $1,334 per year; and $1,000,000+, $32,111 per year.

Similarly, conservatives were lying about what they did to future generations of Americans. For example, on 18 September 2006, *Newsweek*'s Allan Sloan headlined "D.C.'s Deficit Math Doesn't Add Up," and he predicted (which turned out to be correct) that, "Next month the White House and its congressional allies will be taking victory laps when the deficit for fiscal 2006 is announced. The stated deficit for the year, which ends Sept. 30, will be $260 billion or so. That will be down $58 billion from 2005 and a whopping $77 billion below what the nonpartisan Congressional Budget Office predicted in January. ... But let me share a dirty secret with you: the real federal deficit isn't $260 billion. It's more than double that." Sloan explained in simple terms the deception which Republicans would be perpetrating upon the American people: "The stated deficit is the difference between the cash that the government takes in and the cash it spends. That's $260 billion. ... But Uncle Sam will also borrow almost $300 billion from federal trust funds: $177 billion from Social Security, and an additional $121 billion from 'other government accounts.' ... If a company tried to keep books this way, its accountants would scream." This deception by Republicans fooled even liberals, most of whom understood little or nothing about such accounting matters. For example, a month after Sloan's column, the liberal columnist Molly Ivins, on October 24th, headlined "It's Good to Be the Richest of the Rich" and she stated that, "When Bush took over in 2001, he predicted a surplus of $516 billion for fiscal year 2006. Last week, the administration announced a 2006 deficit of $248 billion, missing its projection for this year by $764 billion." However, actually, the situation was far worse than even Ivins understood. Bush was missing *by over a trillion dollars* his 2006 prediction, which he had made in 2001. Republican operatives thus fooled not just conservatives, but also liberals.

On 7 July 2008, Paul Krugman's blog at the website of The New York Times headlined "Bush Boom Bah" and presented the following chart (which was from the CBPP's 22 April 2008 "How Robust Was the 2001-2007 Economic Expansion?"):

It showed "The 2001-2007 Expansion Was Weaker Than Average; Only Corporate Profits Grew Rapidly." Whereas GDP, Consumption, Investment, Income, Wealth, and Employment, all underperformed "Other Post World War II Expansions," Corporate Profits outperformed – it was the only thing that outperformed. So: On 6 of the 7 measures, the Bush expansion was well below average, but on the 7th, which is the only one that aristocrats usually focus upon and depend upon for their stock gains and also for their executive bonuses, the Bush expansion *exceeded* the average. Conservatism benefited aristocrats, while it harmed everyone else.

Nor is this sort of thing unique to America. For example, on 30 March 2006, the *Wall Street Journal* headlined "As Italy Votes, Golden Career Of Berlusconi Is at Crossroads," and reported that, after five years in power, Italy's most successful private businessman was running the Italian national economy into the ground. "Even on this sluggish continent, Italy is an underperformer. Growth last year was zero. Though nominally a free-market conservative, Mr. Berlusconi has done little to break monopolies, including those that keep Italians paying among the highest energy prices in Europe and impose steep fees for opening a business." Americans were dreaming of having someone just like this replace George W. Bush — Berlusconi's American friend. It was the conservative hoax at work.

On July 4th of 2006, which was a Monday, *The New York Times* headlined "Prodi Pushes Liberalization of Italian Industries," and Peter Kiefer reported from Rome: "Prime Minister Romano Prodi [who had just recently defeated electorally the fascist Berlusconi] on Monday held fast to his

plans to liberalize some of Italy's most protected industries."
Conservatives called themselves supporters of business, but
they were actually supporters only of the most corrupt and
inefficient large businesses, against the entire society. This
corruption they called "capitalism"; it was actually fascism.

Just a few months later, on November 24th, the BBC
headlined "Italian Right 'Tried to Rig Poll'," and reported
that, "Italian prosecutors have launched an inquiry into claims
that the government of ex-Prime Minister Silvio Berlusconi
tried to rig April's general elections." The report noted that,
"The official election results gave a razor-thin majority to the
center-left, while opinion and exit polls had suggested Mr
Berlusconi's party would be soundly beaten. ... The authors"
of the new study "suggest that a computer program allowed
the interior ministry to change blank votes." This could just as
well have been a news story about the 2004 U.S. Presidential
election; but instead Italy was the subject.

On 10 December 2006, CBS "60 Minutes" headlined
"Provenzano: The Phantom of Corleone," and reported that
Italian Senator Marcello Dell'Utri, who had worked as
Berlusconi's private secretary, lived in his house, headed one
of his companies, and organized his political party, was one of
the chief lieutenants for the Mafia's top boss, Bernardo
Provenzano.

Fascism has never looked good to people on the
outside. Did Hitler look good to Poles? Of course not. They
detested him. Similarly, on 9 October 2006, *BusinessWeek*
headlined (p. 11) "U.S. Competitiveness: Failing on the
Fundamentals," and reported that during the past year the
United States had fallen in the international competitiveness
rankings by the World Economic Forum at Davos, from first
place to sixth, largely because "The index uses statistics and a
survey of 11,000 business executives worldwide. Dragging
down the U.S. score, besides macroeconomic factors: high
infant mortality, relatively low life expectancy, and poor
marks from the executives on government effectiveness." But
to people on the inside, to Americans, America seemed fine.

Interestingly, "China is only No. 54 among 125 nations,
behind Costa Rica. (It got demerits for its weak banks and
courts.)" Fascist regimes weren't economically more
competitive by virtue of their being controlled by fascists, but
rather *less* competitive. Only to the domestic populations, who
were suckered by the local government's propaganda, did
fascism possess appeal. America's fascist "news" media
generally treated capitalist nations, which were at the very top
of the charts, as being socialist, or somehow *less* free than
America. "The top five: Switzerland, Finland, Sweden,
Denmark, and Singapore — neat and tidy nations where all
the budgets are strong and all the savings rates are above
average." Only in America did those nations appear to be
unfree. But perhaps they were, in fact, more free, and more
advanced, than America. They were less religious, and less
feudal; they were, in important respects, closer to what
America's Founders had hoped this nation would become.

On 22 November 2006, Alan Murray in the *Wall Street
Journal* headlined "Pivotal Fight Looms for Shareholder
Democracy," and he described the struggle stockholders were
engaged in to win the ability to elect corporate directors in
America. Despite widespread Republican-promulgated
myths, corporate elections in America were routinely rigged
from the top. "Until recently, those elections were Stalinesque:
Only one slate of candidates was on the ballot, and while
shareholders could withhold their support, withheld votes
didn't count. ... Three years ago, then-SEC Chairman William
Donaldson picked up the banner of shareholder democracy
and proposed giving shareholders limited ability to nominate
directors. Big Business and the White House forced him to
retreat and, ultimately, to resign. ... Then, last year, the
American Federation of State, County and Municipal
Employees [widely loathed by the Wall Street Journal and the
Republican Party] took a different tack. The big public-
employee union submitted a proxy measure to American
International Group that would change the company's bylaws
to allow shareholders to nominate directors." Donaldson's

successor, Republican Christopher Cox, was now being faced with having to make a decision regarding which the Business Roundtable, and the other groups behind the firing of Donaldson, were going to determine whether Cox himself was going to be in their gunsights. The big change since the last time around was that control of the Congress had swung to the Democrats. Without Democrats in charge in Washington, American outside investors don't stand a chance, and the rigging of stock markets against the public is virtually assured. In a Big Brother country such as was the U.S., it was widely believed that the Republican Party was good for business and that the Democratic Party was bad for business. However, the gangsters at the top knew better: they feared Democrats. And these gangsters enjoyed the faith of religious Americans, whose politics were decided by myths which were driven by fear of death. Thus, the aristocracy and the clergy were united against the public.

On 5 December 2006, the *Wall Street Journal* published two stories which indicated where Bush's SEC under the new Chairman Christopher Cox was heading. "SEC Considers Adjustments To Short-Selling Regulations" discussed limitations the SEC imposed against "short sellers" or stock investors who gambled that share prices would go down, but which the SEC didn't impose against investors who gambled that share prices would go up — thus placing a thumb on the scale in favor of artificially raising the stock market. "SEC Officials to Defend Decisions In Insider-Trading Probe" concerned "Gary Aguirre, a former SEC enforcement attorney. Mr. Aguirre has alleged that he was fired in September 2005 after his supervisors blocked him from issuing subpoenas to John Mack, former chief executive of Credit Suisse First Boston, now head of Morgan Stanley." On 28 June 2006, Aguirre had testified to Congress: "Is federal law enforcement adequately protecting the nation's capital markets and their participants from the risk of manipulation and fraud by the nation's 11,500 hedge funds? The answer is no." His testimony documented this in case after case — for which reason he was

kicked out of the SEC, after having received glowing reviews
from his superiors who were now booting him. The day
before, Felix Gillette at cjrdaily.org headlined "Will the Media
Blow Off a Whistleblower?" and noted that the major media
had studiously avoided reporting on Aguirre's charge against
the SEC, and had instead reported only on problems at hedge
funds. On 23 June 2006, thesanitycheck.com, written by an
anonymous "veteran investor" and "shareholder activist"
who was anonymous because he feared certain "criminal
elements" on Wall Street, bannered "Must Read Documents
— The Ugly Truth About the SEC?" and he said: "A former
SEC staffer [Mr. Aguirre] wrote two landmark letters
highlighting what can only be described as obvious
corruption of the Commission, and the sort of cover-up" that
is supposed to occur only "in third world countries." Aguirre's
letter to Christopher Cox described why Aguirre feared for
"the integrity of the financial markets and to protect the
investor," and described "an institutional form of insider
trading that corrupts the financial markets and creates an un-
level playing field for honest investors."

  Mr. Cox waited until the Christmas/New-Year's break
to lower the boom on outside investors. On 27 December 2006,
the "Naked Shorts" website of Greg Newton headlined,
appropriately, "The Crooks Are Running the Reformatory,"
and he linked to that day's blockbuster story from Floyd
Norris of *The New York Times*, "S.E.C. Changes Reporting Rule
on Bosses' Pay," which opened: "The Securities and Exchange
Commission, in a move announced late on the last business
day before Christmas, reversed a decision it had made in July
and adopted a rule that would allow many companies to
report significantly lower total compensation for top
executives. The change in the way grants of stock options are
to be explained to investors is a victory for [top executives of]
corporations that had opposed the rule when it was issued in
July, and a defeat for institutional investors that had opposed
the rule. 'It was a holiday present to corporate America,' Ann

Yerger, the executive director of the Council of Institutional Investors, said yesterday. 'It will certainly make the number look smaller in 2007 than they would otherwise have looked.' Christopher Cox, the commission chairman, said yesterday that he viewed the decision as 'a relative technicality.'"

On 27 March 2007, the *Wall Street Journal* bannered "Securities Suits on Trial," and presented a chart, "Less Litigation: Number of federal securities-fraud class-action filings," which showed that the Bush Administration's filings of these suits blipped up in 2001, returned to the norm immediately in 2002, and stayed there till 2004, after which (with the media's attention averted) they plunged.

The very next day, on the 28th, the *WSJ* headlined "Wall Street Appeals to High Court," and reported that, "The Supreme Court appeared inclined to give Wall Street firms another shot at deflecting a class-action lawsuit claiming they illegally drove up prices and margins on initial public offerings during the 1990s bubble. ... The high court heard pleas from more than a dozen Wall Street underwriters and brokerages that are seeking broad immunization from a lawsuit filed on behalf of investors in about 900 technology and internet firms." During oral arguments on the 27th, in the case *Credit Suisse v. Billing*, the conservative "Justice"s seemed sympathetic to investment banks claiming that they possessed "implied antitrust immunity," so that, as Wall Street's lawyer put it to the Court, on behalf of the "Petitioners," "there would be serious problems if antitrust law were applied to these allegations," and moreover that this was true regardless of one's "position on the merit of the underlying claims" from investors. Scalia said that the cost which would be entailed in pursuing Wall Street firms who conspired to fix the price of an initial public offering "isn't worth the candle." The attorney for the investors replied, "Your honor, I think you have — for the good of the country — I think you have to follow the facts and find out if these people conspired as alleged." Chief "Justice" John Roberts interjected that such a conspiracy "is exactly what the SEC wants. ... They want them to agree on an appropriate IPO price that's going to contribute to capital formation." "Justice" Roberts assumed that conspiracies to jack up stock prices are good for "capital formation" — that the way to boost "capital formation" is to exploit, instead of to serve, outside investors. The investors' lawyer replied that, even if this were true, "you don't go over and rig the after market, not even in one stock, let alone what we allege, across stocks." Basically, the Wall Street and Bush Administration position was that SEC regulation meant that antitrust laws don't apply to the securities industry. The Chief "Justice," in effect, was going even further than that, and asserting that SEC regulation of the industry *demands* exactly what antitrust laws *prohibit*, so that Wall Street was merely doing its duty by conspiring to jack up IPO prices and conspiring to keep them up. John Roberts was saying, in effect, that a regulatory agency represents the interests not of consumers (in this case, of investors) but of producers (in this case, of IPO firms and investment banks and major mutual fund groups). Roberts's underlying assumption has been called "supply-side economics" in another context; and this economic theory came to the fore during the Reagan Administration, which had initially brought Roberts into the government. Both Roberts and Reagan were highly regarded by the American public in 2007. The view that Roberts expressed was not considered to be fascistic or otherwise extreme, but simply, at worst, bad luck for some investors who had experienced huge losses in 1990's-era investments. The investors who were suing in this case were outside investors. Giant mutual-fund organizations and other major inside investment firms were among the targets of this lawsuit. All of the 42 people suing had obscure names, such as Glen Billing, Mita Aggarwal, and Henry Sklanowsky, as well as Joe Goldgrab and Local 144 Nursing Home Pension Fund. None of them had contributed huge sums to the Republican Party — nor to any party. The 17 defendants, by contrast, included 7 of the 20 "Top Contributors" to "George W. Bush" for "All Cycles" as shown at opensecrets.org, and few of the major Wall Street firms were absent from this list of 17 defendants. A better exemplar of weak versus powerful would be hard to find; and a tribal and religious America seemed set to crush the little guys in this case. After all, The Almighty was worshipped.

Barely a week later, on 6 April 2007, *Wall Street Journal* columnist Kimberly A. Strassel headlined "Judging the Bush Legacy," and she said that, though President Bush's quantitative contribution to reforming the courts had unfortunately been limited by Democratic obstructionism, "What voters have appreciated more has been the White House's rigorous attention to judicial philosophy (no Souters here!). [Supreme Court Justice David Souter was one of the few Republican appointees who voted against the conservatives in most cases.] ... The payoff was two stellar Supreme Court successes — John Roberts and Sam Alito." Strassel likewise praised many Bush-appointed "appellate all-stars." Opinion polls consistently indicated that the American public strongly supported the appointment of conservative, and not of progressive, judges. Americans supported Biblical Law, but weren't favorably inclined toward constitutional Law in a democratic nation. Given the choice, Americans overwhelmingly preferred and trusted the Bible over the U.S. Constitution, and they wanted jurists with similar power-worshipping sensibilities. The aristocracy existed in order to put people in their places, and a religious American society respected aristocrats, and wanted aristocrats to pick their sinning pockets — no riff-raff mere street-level crooks for such a job!

Ten days later, on April 16th, the *WSJ* headlined "SEC Explores Opening Door To Arbitration," and Kara Scannell reported that, "The Securities and Exchange Commission is exploring a new policy that could permit companies to resolve complaints by aggrieved shareholders through arbitration, limiting shareholders' ability to sue in court. ... The idea of giving companies the option of arbitrating shareholder disputes is likely to spark fierce opposition from both investor-rights groups and trial lawyers." This proposal, if approved by the SEC, would give corporations the right to bar stockholders from suing, and to force stockholders into arbitration, which would be more directly beholden to corporate executives, and be less able to hold executives accountable for stealing from outside investors. Even after voters had replaced a Republican Congress with a Democratic one, George W. Bush was pushing new aristocratic frontiers.

However, the old feudal social order that America's great Founders tried to overthrow, and that the Republican Party has re-installed, is a drag, not a propellant, to a nation's economy and culture. Yet the fear of death is a potent motive in any society, and so religious myths die hard — very hard, and very slowly. Since the fear of death is the ultimate fear, it is also the ultimate source for conservatism's enduring popularity.

Thus the Chicago *Tribune* bannered on Thursday, 21 June 2007, "Investors Have More to Prove in Fraud Suits: High Court Decides in Favor of Tellabs," and reported that, "In a closely watched case that centered on Naperville-based Tellabs Inc., the U.S. Supreme Court on Thursday issued a ruling that will make it significantly harder for shareholders to file securities-fraud suits against corporations. ... Investor groups ... predicted the 8-1 ruling will make it harder than ever for defrauded stockholders to get their rightful day in court." From now on, investors wouldn't even be able to *file* a suit alleging a knowingly false earnings forecast by executives, unless those investors *first* proved that the executives *knew* the forecast to be false. Only in such cases could the suit be permitted to be heard by a court in order to determine whether or not the false statements had, indeed, been knowingly false. Instead of stockholders needing to prove the executive(s)' guilt once, they would now have to prove it twice, in order to win. Several of the Democratic Justices joined in this majority decision (and Democrat Ruth Ginsburg in fact wrote it), because an alternative decision by Scalia and Alito would have weakened investors' rights even more. The only Justice dissenting against this decision, *Tellabs v. Makor*, was Democrat John Paul Stevens — and this dissent was itself weak, alleging that the majority's decision was "perfectly workable" but that he had "a different interpretion." Chief judge John Roberts, of course, joined in the majority opinion.

Three days earlier, on 18 June 2007, *Credit Suisse v. Billing* was decided. This was the case testing whether SEC regulation of securities brokers prohibited cheated investors from suing their brokers who had conspired against their interests. Shockingly, the only Justice who rendered a decision favorable to investors on this was Clarence Thomas. All of the others, even the jurists who had been appointed by a Democratic President, favored the fascistic "free market" view, that less regulation is always better regulation. Clarence Thomas's dissent noted that the Securities Act of 1933 contained a clause specifically protecting the rights of cheated investors to sue their cheating brokers, even where the SEC hasn't barred those brokers from cheating. The only decent jurist on this case in the U.S. Supreme Court was Thomas. This was the most uncharacteristic decision ever from Thomas. Was this a temporary insanity, or a philosophical turnaround for him?

On 6 October 2005, William Taylor headlined in the *New York Review of Books*, "The Nominee," and documented that during the Reagan Administration John Roberts had opposed the extremely conservative Administration lawyers Theodore Olson and Robert Bork because they weren't sufficiently extreme in their support for granting dictatorial powers to the Presidency. Roberts's position on blocking Blacks from voting was likewise far to the Right. And yet even many liberal legal scholars backed the congenial John Roberts's nomination to the U.S. Supreme Court. During the subsequent twenty years the nation had moved so extremely far to the Right that what had formerly seemed *too* far ended up sitting in the seat of the Chief "Justice" of the United States.

Conservatives always favor the powerful over the weak. However, sometimes the weak are actually more efficient, and sometimes the powerful are the effective *block* against increasing efficiency. This can happen especially when the powerful represent old technologies, and the weak represent challenging new technologies. On 23 July 2007, economist and *New York Times* columnist Paul Krugman headlined "The French Connections," and he documented that broadband connections in the U.S. — which was the former leader — were now falling increasingly behind the rest of the world. "As recently as 2001, the percentage of the population with high-speed access in Japan and Germany was only half that in the United States. In France it was less than a quarter. By the end of 2006, however, all three countries had more broadband subscribers per 100 people than we did."

An interesting letter to the editor of the *Wall Street Journal* appeared on 2 October 2007, responding to the argument which had previously been given in that newspaper by Professor Lynn Stout opposing corporate democracy, and favoring, as did the newspaper itself, dictatorship in corporate governance. Solomon Moshkevich of Boston said: "Prof. Stout's argument is built on the false premise that the size of a corporation is testament to its success and that the fact that a high number of the world's 30 largest corporations are located in the U.S. proves the quality of its corporate law." Numerous empirical studies have shown that large corporations, as a lot, are less efficient, not more efficient, than medium-sized ones. The only reason why fascists equate large size with high efficiency is that this equation suits their anti-scientific version of Darwinism, "social Darwinism." But in reality, large firms are like large animals, and in Darwinian theory there is no advantage for large animals as a group. Cockroaches might have far more advantages than do elephants. Republicans favor large corporations for the same reason that they favor control of corporations by corporate insiders and not by stockholders. But such false ideology doesn't promote, it diminishes, the performance of a nation's economy.

On 17 December 2007, Carol Hymowitz's "In the Lead" column in the *Wall Street Journal* headlined "Companies Need CEOs To Stop Spinning And Start Thinking," and she discussed what makes for a successful big-corporate CEO: "'Successful executives have to be able to discern the really important decisions and get a high percentage of them right,' says Warren Bennis, a professor at the University of Southern California and co-author with Noel Tichy of 'Judgment: How Winning Leaders Make Great Calls.' 'This is the heart of great leadership.'" This, and *not* psychopathy and ruthlessness which are embodied by charm, good looks, charisma, and a network of personal connections amongst people relevant to advancing the striver's career. Of course, there do exist a few CEO's such as Bennis fantasied, but that's hardly the corporate CEO norm. Bennis exhibited raw faith in the "invisible hand" of God, and so served the *actual* devils of this world, and advanced the Republican myth.

The reality was publicized in May 2011 when Jon Ronson's *The Psychopath Test* was published, about Bob Hare and his "PCL-R Test," which had established extraordinarily high predictive value regarding whether or not a released-from-prison criminal would commit more crimes. This personality test for psychopathy produced high scores not only on convicted psychopaths, but also on many CEO's and corporate directors, extremely successful people, such as Al Dunlap, the "Chainsaw Al" who famously went from one corporation to another firing large numbers of employees so as to drive the stock price up. Big-corporate leaders score high for psychopathy. The Republican Party was run by them, for them, and elected by the masses of faithful.

Faith continued to reign. On 16 April 2008, immediately after the Pennsylvania Democratic Presidential primary debate between Hillary Clinton and Barack Obama, Chris Cillizza's "The Fix" blog headlined "The Closing Statements" and a viewer commented there, with outrage, against Barack Obama's statement that tax rates on dividends and on capital gains should be the same as on wages, 28%, which used to be the case but no longer was: the current rate under G.W. Bush was 15%. Someone commented there: "I'm not a shill for Clinton. In fact, I'm an independent. But as a middle class person (who does own stocks!) I was really perturbed about what Obama said. Is this a long-term position of his? What I got is that Obama is willing to raise my taxes even though it won't help the country. I might not mind paying higher taxes to help the country. I do mind paying higher taxes because some secretary is jealous [of his/her boss, presumably the writer]!" That commentator had faith in trickle-down economic theory, and so accepted unquestioningly the conservative propaganda that taxes on investment-income hurt long-term economic growth, whereas taxes on labor-income don't. It's nothing more than worship of The Almighty. "Jealousy" had nothing to do with the issue. This comment was, in fact, being made six years after President Bush had lowered capital gains tax-rates from 20% down to 15%, and had left taxes on wages at 28%; and yet the growth-rate in real private investment since that change had actually plunged, from 5.46% down to the current rate of 1.01%. So, such a comment required lots of faith — in propaganda from the aristocracy. Essentially, that commentator personally identified his interests with those of the aristocracy, rather than with those of workers. He possessed the faith that he was one of God's People.

        This commentator was following up on anti-Obama propaganda from Charlie Gibson, the conservative multimillionaire ABC news anchor and debate moderator, who, at this Democratic primary debate, had pressed Senator Obama at length on Obama's proposed tax-hikes for the wealthy, especially on his proposed capital-gains tax-rate hike (back to the former 28% cap-gains tax-rate). "That's almost a doubling if you went [back] to 28 percent," exclaimed Gibson, with apparent dread. Gibson, owning a substantial stock portfolio himself, praised President Bush for having lowered the cap-gains tax-rate to 15%. "And in each instance when the rate dropped, revenues from the tax increased," said this debate "moderator." (This conservative propagandist ignored the huge and soaring Bush deficits.) Obama objected, but Gibson restated his attack against Hillary Clinton's debate-opponent: "But history shows that when you drop the capital gains tax, the revenues go up." What Gibson said was false. Of course, short-term, the revenues from this tax do increase after a rate-cut, but not because the rate-cut produces greater investment (such as conservatives claim) — it's because the first thing that lowering the cap-gains tax-rate does is to unleash increased sales of *existing* taxable appreciated stocks. Because of this cap-gains rate-cut, more sellers of appreciated stocks are *brought into the market*. This floods the stock market. These are pent-up stock-sales, all of which had been postponed in order to defer the tax-liability, under the old, higher, tax-rate. The lowered tax-rate suddenly makes these stock-sales far more attractive; they're more attractive *because of* the new lower taxation-rate. Bringing more sellers into the market, however — since the tax-rate-decline does *nothing* to increase *purchases* of stocks, nothing to bring increased numbers of *buyers* into the stock market — the stock market itself actually *goes down*. (This is just basic economics: raising the number of sellers, without raising the number of buyers, inevitably *lowers* the price-level on the thing that's being sold. It's called *the law of supply and demand*.) Tax-collections thus rise in the *immediate* wake of a cap-gains cut, because these taxable cap-gains are being realized during the resulting immediate *burst* of stock-sales, sales which would otherwise have been simply *postponed*. But tax-collections in *future* years consequently plunge, due not only to this lowering of the tax-rate, but to the very fact that the earlier burst of stock-selling has already released part of stocks' capital gains; the tax on that portion of gains was already paid in the first year after the selling-burst. The decline in tax-collections to the federal treasury that's produced by the rate-cut *itself*, is thus exacerbated by that earlier stock-selling burst, which has already depleted part of stocks' taxable gains. That's why Republican "supply-side economics" is so widely recognized by economists as being a hoax, and even under conservative Republican presidents and congresses, federal "scoring" doesn't assume that reducing any tax-rate "pays for itself." Furthermore, on 18 May 2006, Knight Ridder Newspapers bannered "Tax Cuts Lose More Money Than They Generate, Studies Conclude," and reported that even President Bush's Treasury Secretary and chief economists *acknowledged* that the idea that these tax cuts produce "more revenue for the federal treasury" are "just not true." It's a pure conservative hoax, a lie to get suckers to vote for the interests of the super-rich.

For a smug rich conservative like Gibson, propagandizing in favor of Republican policies wasn't merely an expression of his faith; it was an expression of his self-interest as an aristocrat, who might actually benefit from continuing the transference of the nation's tax-burden from investors onto workers. But for the Cillizza respondent, the commentator on Cillizza's website who was "really perturbed" about the prospect of raising the cap-gains rate back up to the 28% tax-rate that prevailed on wage income, such continuance of the prejudice favoring cap-gains over wage-income might not be in his interest; and, in any case, the assumption that a way to reduce the federal deficit *long-term* is to reduce the cap-gains tax-rate isn't just false; it's downright stupid. It violates the basic law of economics: supply and demand. So, it requires lots of faith, because it's the exact *opposite* of the truth.

However, lots of Pennsylvanians possessed faith: on 21 April 2008, the eve of the Pennsylvania primary, Suffolk University headlined "Poll: Clinton Headed for Keystone State Win," and reported that when 600 registered Democrats who intended to vote in this Democratic primary were asked "Are you in favor of tax increases to help close the budget deficit gap?" 65% said "No," and only 27% said "Yes." And these respondents were Democrats; *not* Republicans. They didn't realize that the tax increases would be only on aristocrats, not on people like themselves. They didn't realize that Bush's tax-cuts, which had caused the huge federal deficits, were cuts almost *only* for the aristocracy. Even Democrats didn't want aristocrats to pay higher taxes. They felt this way, even though failing to increase, back to the 28%, the taxation-rate upon capital gains, would mean that *their own children* would thereby inherit a financially wrecked, if not outright bankrupt, country, just to provide added benefits to today's aristocracy.

All Americans were inundated with this pro-aristocrat propaganda, which alleged that raising the cap-gains rate, so as to equalize it to the tax-rate that prevailed on labor-based wages, would hurt rather than help the average American. Rupert Murdoch's *New York Post* headlined Richard Johnson's "Page Six" column on 10 June 2008, attacking "Barack's Bite" against readers' (such as against Rupert Murdoch's own) wallets, and featured CNBC's Maria Bartiromo (hardly a poor person herself) warning: "He's going to take the capital gains tax at 15 percent right now all the way up to 25 to 28 percent. ... It's actually going to impact more people than you may think."

On the very next day's Fox "News" Channel "Fox & Friends" (another Murdoch-outlet), Ben Stein, a prominent Hollywood Republican and a New York Times business columnist who was the son of President Richard Nixon's Council of Economic Advisers Chairman Herb Stein, said that under Obama's plan, viewers' retirement savings are "going to be taxed away, your retirement is in severe jeopardy. So I'm very worried about increasing the capital gains tax, unless you want to just increase it on people that are terribly wealthy. I have no problem with increasing the tax on people who have an income of $5 million a year or more." However, this figure, "$5 million a year or more," represented actually the top 0.01% (hundredth of one percent) of American incomes: On 5 June 2005, David Cay Johnston had headlined in *The New York Times*, "Richest Are Leaving Even the Rich Far Behind" and he reported that, "the uppermost 0.01 percent (now about 14,000 households, each with $5.5 million or more in income last year)," were "the hyper-rich." Stein's characterization of himself, and of other such aristocrats, as being merely Joe-public was a fraud upon the public. Mediamatters.org headlined the next day, "Who Misrepresented Obama's Tax Plan? Anyone? Ben Stein," and reported: "In fact, Obama has said he would not raise the capital gains tax on individuals with income of less than $250,000." That's hardly "$5 million a year or more." So, America's major "news" media worked overtime to deceive suckers to fear Obama and to vote for Hillary Clinton, and, subsequently for the Republican candidate John McCain.

How would Obama's plan *really* affect the average Pennsylvanian, or the average American? On 20 June 2008, the Tax Policy Center of the Brookings Institution and of the Urban Institute, headlined "A Preliminary Analysis of the 2008 Presidential Candidates' Tax Plans," and reported that by 2012 Obama's plan would lower taxes the most for the poorest, and would raise taxes virtually *only* on the top 1% — raise their taxes by 3%, and it would raise taxes by 5% *on the top tenth of 1%*. Obama's plan would actually *reduce* taxes by about 6% for the poorest 20%, decrease 6% for the second-poorest 20%, decrease 5% for the middle 20%, decrease 4% for the next 20%, and decrease 1% for the top 20%. By contrast, McCain's plan would produce less than a meager 1% decrease in taxes for the bottom 20%, decrease only 3% for the next 20%, decrease only 4% for the middle 20%, decrease 5% for the next 20%, and decrease 6% for the top 20%. McCain would decrease taxes by 10% for the top 1%, and by a very substantial 12% for the top tenth of 1%.

So, it's no wonder that the conservative multi-millionaires, Charlie Gibson and Ben Stein, were hostile towards Obama.* But lots of Americans had faith in Power,

---

* Mr. Stein suddenly became a populist on the day of the $700 billion Wall Street bailout agreement in Congress, on 28 September 2008, when he headlined in *The New York Times*, "In Financial Firms, Little Guys Can't Win," and he

and so they identified with these self-obsessed aristocrats, as they attacked Obama — such as Mr. Gibson did when serving as the supposed "moderator" of this supposed debate, which was supposed to be *between Hillary Clinton and Barack Obama* for the Democratic Presidential nomination in 2008, and not between Obama and the debate's moderator/inquisitor. It required lots of sheer faith to view this ABC debate *between Gibson and Obama* as being an actual debate between the candidates. The medium was the message, and aristocrats

---

expressed outrage there at U.S. Treasury Secretary Henry Paulson and "at what the traders, speculators, hedge funds and the government have done to everyone who is saving and investing for retirement and future security. Millions of us did nothing wrong, according to the accepted wisdom of the age. We saved. We put a large part of our money into the stock market, as we were urged to do. ... Now we have the rug pulled out from under us. Our retirements have been put into severe jeopardy." He lambasted rapacious financial executives, but especially Paulson, and he urged many of the policies that Democrats had been urging to be included in this legislation, but which Stein's fellow-Republicans had actually blocked, such as renegotiation of these distressed mortgages, saying such things as, "Maybe the bailout should not be of the banks at all, but of homeowners themselves," just as if he were a Democrat.

This fake populist urged many other positions that Democratic Presidential candidate Barack Obama, and Democrats in Congress, had long been urging, and some of which the Democrats now managed to get the Republicans in Congress and the Republican Presidential candidate, John McCain, to agree to, and to include in this legislation. But the fake populist avoided mentioning that what he was now writing was actually just standard Democratic pronouncements, and that these policies had always been blocked by his fellow Republicans.

Sometimes, even fascists urge progressive policies, after coming out on the losing end themselves of the policies they've always supported. But this blathering doesn't usually transform such a fascist into a democrat. It typically reflects, instead, merely a disgruntled and hypocritical fascist.

This was reminiscent of when Stein had promoted his biblical-creationist movie on Paul Crouch's and Jim and Tammy Bakker's Trinity Broadcasting Network, on 21 April 2008, by saying that "science leads you to killing people," even though he had earlier written in *The New York Times*, on 26 November 2006, that such views as Dick Cheney's famous "Deficits don't matter" reflected "what doctors call magical thinking." The full sentence he spoke on TBN was: "Love of God and compassion and empathy leads you to a very glorious place, and science leads you to killing people." Was *this* "magical thinking"?

Some people are just professional hypocrites.

controlled the media. The millions of people who fell for their line were just suckers.

The first major mass-mailing of the McCain-for-President general-election operation showed up in millions of U.S. mailboxes during mid-July of 2008, and it included a 10-question "Stand Up For America Survey," in which the recipient was to choose between McCain and Obama. The *first* question in this "Survey" (which was actually nothing but a fundraising piece) opened by stating that, "Senator Obama has advocated raising taxes." It omitted mentioning that only earners of more than $250K/yr. would experience an increase under Obama's plan; and it also omitted mentioning this plan's tax-*decreases* for *everyone below that income*.

On 10 August 2008, a *Washington Post* editorial headlined "To Listen Is Taxing," and these editors excoriated a McCain TV commercial which misleadingly alleged that "Obama voted to raise taxes on people making just $42,000." The newspaper's editors then wrote, "The McCain ad continues in the same dishonest vein: 'He promises more taxes on small businesses, seniors, your life savings, your family.' Mr. Obama would increase taxes on small business — but only the tiny sliver that earn more than $250,000 a year. He would — unwisely, in our view — lower taxes on seniors, excusing those making less than $50,000 a year from paying any tax whatsoever." And this editorial listed other McCain lies concerning Obama's tax plan.

However, by now, Obama's poll numbers were heading toward a very tight Presidential contest with McCain, and it was becoming clear that Obama would no longer be able to maintain such a high ground on tax-fairness and on fiscal soundness. He would have to pander — not to poor people but to the rich, and also to middle class fools who fantasized that they were going to become rich and that the interests of middle class individuals aren't as important as the interests of the rich. He modified his tax-plan. On August 14th, two top Obama economic advisors, Jason Furman and Austan Goolsbee, headlined a *Wall Street Journal* op-ed "The

Obama Tax Plan," and presented his new plan, without noting that it was different from what he had been proposing previously. However, these economists admitted, as if it were hardly worth mentioning, that, """his middle-class tax cuts are larger than the rollbacks he has proposed for families making over $250,000." This hadn't been the case with Obama's original plan. The following day, the *New York Sun* bannered "Obama Aides Say He Would Lower Taxes," and Russell Berman reported that, "Senator Obama, with his lead against Senator McCain narrowing in some polls, is trying to portray himself as the real tax-cutter in the presidential race," as if Obama hadn't been that all along, for all but the highest-income 2%. Berman likewise failed to report that Obama had modified his tax-plan so as to reduce its hit on aristocrats, but Berman simply noted that, "A senior policy analyst at the conservative Heritage Foundation, Rea Hederman Jr., praised Mr. Obama for proposing a 20% tax rate on dividends and capital gains, lower than a 28% rate he had initially floated, though still more than the current 15% rate. 'That's a great step in the right direction,' Mr. Hederman said. 'It's a big change from" Obama's original tax plan. "Mr. Hederman said the middle class would likely pay less under Mr. Obama's [new] plan than under Mr. McCain's." That fact, however, had been equally true before Obama had caved to the fascist "liberal" media, fascist think tanks, and the other Republican pressure-groups, and lowered his proposed cap-gains and dividend tax-rate to 20%, from his original 28% proposal. Then, the very next day, on the 16th, *The New York Times* headlined "Obama Camp Puts Forward More Modest Tax Changes" and Larry Rohter reported: "Senator Barack Obama appears to be altering his proposals for extending Social Security payroll taxes and raising the capital gains tax." Howard Gleckman, the editor of the TaxVox blog at the Tax Policy Center, was quoted there as saying that, "nothing ... is left of Barack Obama's plan to fix Social Security" through extending the 12.4% Social Security tax to earnings above $97,500/year as they were limited under the current law.

Obama would now essentially continue the existing limitation of SS taxes to only earnings lower than that figure. Obama's tax-policy changes were attributed to "a desire not to alienate affluent and wealthy voters," but his campaign responded by saying that "he wants to protect middle-class families," thus implicitly accepting the myth that people such as Charlie Gibson and Ben Stein had been promulgating about his tax-plan. Obama could no longer hold out against this myth.

America's major news media continued their war against Obama's effort to remove Bush's tax-favoritism of the rich. For example, the AP's Charles Babington "reported" on Obama's speech accepting the Democratic Presidential nomination, and headlined on 29 August 2008, "Analysis: Obama Spares Details, Keeps Up Attacks." In this "analysis" of a speech which was widely received as being the most specific on policy details, and also the best Presidential-nomination-acceptance speech, ever, Babington said, snidely, "For instance, Obama said it's time 'to protect Social Security for future generations.' But he didn't mention his main [oh, 'main'?] proposal, which is to add a new Social Security payroll tax to incomes above $250,000 a year." Then, an honest journalist responded: America's leading critic of the aristocratic slant of the nation's newspapers, Greg Mitchell, who was the editor of *Editor & Publisher*, headlined "MSNBC Host Rips AP Reporter's Analysis of Obama Speech," and Mitchell noted that not only Babington, but also the AP's Ron Fournier and Jim Drinkard, had been reporting on the Presidential race with a decided slant against Obama. The AP was one of America's major news media, and it reflected a cooperative of the aristocrats who own newspapers around the country. The vast majority of these aristocrats received much of their income from capital gains and dividends, and didn't want this income to be taxed at as high a percentage-rate as were the wages that they paid their reporters and other employees.

The idea of taxing capital gains and dividends at the same percentage as the rate that's paid by workers, was simply not acceptable to the aristocracy — and Americans possessed faith in the aristocracy. Obama needed to set aristocrats more at ease, and so he made these two big concessions to them (cap-gains, and SS), in order to salvage his chances of winning the Presidency. America's future fiscal deficits and debt would suffer from these two concessions. Politics is the art of the possible — not of the best — and Obama knew that the U.S. public treated such people as Gibson and Stein, and as the Heritage Foundation, as being authorities, instead of as the gangsters that they really were, gangsters who used government policy to steal from the masses, and to impoverish succeeding generations of Americans. In other words: traitors.

However, the Washington Post finally had had enough of McCain's deceptions on Obama's tax plan, and, on August 31st, this newspaper ran an editorial headlined "Continuing Deception: Mr. McCain's Ads on Taxes Are Just Plain False." This editorial referred to the latest study from the Tax Policy Center. Titled "An Updated Analysis of the 2008 Presidential Candidates' Tax Plans: Revised August 15, 2008," this study showed that, even with the recent changes which were made in Obama's plan, it was still extremely progressive. People in the lowest quintile (20%) would gain 5.5% in after-tax income immediately, and would gain 7.5% by 2012. The top 0.1% (top tenth of 1%) would see their after-tax income *fall* by 8.9% (in other words, they'd see their taxes *rise*) immediately and they'd see their after-tax income fall by 2.7% by 2012. Everyone but the top 5% would have higher after-tax income immediately, and everyone but the top 1% would have higher after-tax income by 2012. By contrast, the immediate impact of McCain's plan would be a less than 1% rise in after-tax income for everyone in the bottom 60% (people who would be gaining anywhere from 2.6% to 5.5% under Obama's plan), a 1.4% rise for the next quintile (who would be gaining 1.8% under Obama), and the largest immediate gains in McCain's plan would be 4.7%, for the top 0.1%. By 2012, the McCain plan would boost after-tax income for the top 0.1% by a whopping

11.6% (these same people whose after-tax incomes under
Obama would *fall* by 2.7%). One of the huge differences in the
two tax plans would be estate taxes, which would be reduced
within ten years by almost $600 billion under McCain, and by
almost $300 billion under Obama. Under the Obama plan,
only the largest 8,000 estates, those larger than $3.5 million,
would be taxed, at a flat 45% taxation-rate. This would be the
highest taxation-rate in the entire Obama plan, and this fact
demonstrated Obama's recognition that unearned income
must be taxed at a higher rate than any earned income. Under
the McCain plan, only estates larger than $5 million would be
taxed, at a flat 15% rate. The aristocrat McCain was here
proving that he felt that aristocrats should be privileged by
having the lowest taxation-rates of anyone. The reason that
Republicans hammered against Obama's proposed increase in
capital gains taxes (rather than estate taxes) was that
economists offered no substantial case at all against estate
taxes, even while offering their fake "supply-side" case
against capital-gains taxes. How remarkable it is that
economists argue against taxing cap-gains, but *not* against
taxing wages! This exhibits their faith in Power, and it proves
that economists aren't scientists at all. Some economists are
liberals, but none are scientists, because the basis for science
(lack of faith) doesn't exist yet in that area of investigation; the
prejudices favoring power are still dominant there.

　　　Many economists continued to assert that the McCain
tax plan would be better for the economy, even though the
Tax Policy Center's analysis showed that McCain's plan
would increase the national debt by $4.17 trillion over ten
years. (By contrast, the revised Obama plan would increase it
by $2.95 trillion, and the original Obama plan had been set to
raise it by $2.80 trillion. The national debt was bound to go up,
on account of the need to spend government money in order
to get the moribund Bush-Republican economy moving again.
Everyone knows that during an economic recession or
depression, it's economically suicidal to pursue as the primary
goal a reduction in the federal debt.) In other words, McCain's

plan wasn't worse merely from the standpoint of economic equality; it was also worse from the standpoint of the federal debt. And yet many economists preferred the McCain plan to the Obama plan. This, too, exhibited economists' faith in Power.

Two economists especially were influential in forming McCain's tax plan: Douglas Holtz-Eakin, the former Chief Economist for George W. Bush's Council of Economic Advisors; and Phil Gramm, a 12-year economics professor at Texas A&M University who went on to become elected U.S. Senator from Texas. Gramm was furthermore a longtime close personal friend of his Republican Senate colleague, Arizona's John McCain.

Late during the 2008 Presidential campaign, McCain took to smearing Obama with TV commercials tying Obama to an Obama acquaintance, the 1960's leftist radical William Ayers. On 6 October 2008, columnist Harold Meyerson in the *Washington Post*, headlined "A Pal Around McCain," which suggested that if Ayers should be a reason to vote against Obama, then Phil Gramm should certainly be even more of a reason to vote against McCain. Meyerson explained why:

"Gramm was always Wall Street's man in the Senate. As chairman of the Senate Banking Committee during the Clinton administration, he consistently underfunded the Securities and Exchange Commission and kept it from stopping accounting firms from auditing corporations with which they had conflicts of interest. Gramm's piece de resistance came on Dec. 15, 2000, when he slipped into an omnibus spending bill a provision called the Commodity Futures Modernization Act (CFMA), which prohibited any governmental regulation of credit default swaps, those insurance policies covering losses on securities in the event they went belly up. As the housing bubble ballooned, the face value of those swaps rose to a tidy $62 trillion. And as the housing bubble burst, those swaps became a massive pile of worthless paper, because no government agency had required the banks to set aside money to back them up.

"The CFMA also prohibited government regulation of the energy-trading market, which enabled Enron to nearly bankrupt the state of California before bankrupting itself."

Economists had faith in trickle-down, but not in percolate-up, economics. "Supply-side economics" was the power-worshipping norm among economists. This is why the Republican "spin" on Obama's tax plan was that it would depress economic output by promoting welfare for the poor at the expense of "the productive members of society."

For example, one of George W. Bush's speechwriters was Noam Neusner, whose father, the religiously and politically conservative Jew Jacob Neusner, was one of the world's most respected religious scholars. On 3 September 2008, Noam Neusner and Bush economist Al Hubbard co-authored an op-ed in the *Wall Street Journal*, titled "Why Obama Can't Close the Sale," and they wrote: "Mr. Obama's tax plan is a welfare giveaway. ... How so? He would authorize a hodge-podge of refundable tax credits covering everything from education, mortgage payments, child care and other items for people who do not pay income taxes now." Obama was aiming to expand the existing negative income tax, or Earned Income Tax Credit, which had originated with Democratic Senator George McGovern and had been adopted by McGovern's Republican opponent Richard Nixon during the 1970's. This EITC was intended as a replacement of the bureaucracy-laden welfare system, and was directed not only at reducing inequality by providing essential income to the poor, but at getting money into the hands of the very same people who must *spend* it immediately on essentials instead of "*invest*" it (short-term and/or long-term) in corporate stock and other speculative "investments." Not supply-side, it was demand-side economics: percolating economic activity upward from the bottom, rather than trickling economic activity downward from the top. How natural this was, then, when the aristocrats (and the many economists and other propagandists in their employ) dismissed Obama's tax-plan as "a welfare giveaway." Neusner and Hubbard condemned Obama for his "proposed massive tax increase on investors, business owners, and the 'wealthy.'" By their placing that last word in quotation-marks, they were insinuating that within George W. Bush's America, the average person is what Obama was really referring to when he said that his plan would raise taxes only on the "wealthy." The idea here was to scare people that they would experience higher taxes under Obama. Presumably, lots of readers of this newspaper, the *WSJ*, whose average reader made $300,000 yearly and was in the top 2% nationally in terms of income, felt that Obama was aiming to gore their ox; and he was claiming to — but they were *not* "average" Americans; they really *were* wealthy, and trickle-down (or supply-side) economics does *not* produce a thriving national economy. The majority of economists possessed faith in trickle-down (supply-side) not in percolate-up (demand-side) economics, but faith is *not* science. And faith lies.

   This is the reason why, even in a collapsing national U.S. economy after seven years of solid Republican rule, Democrats in the 2008 political campaigns were only modestly favored by Americans for handling the economy. For example, on 10 September 2008, Gallup headlined "On Economy, McCain Gains Ground on Obama," and reported that the two Presidential candidates were almost tied on the question of which one "would better handle" economic matters. (Obama got 48%; McCain got 45%.) Similarly, a CBS poll issued on 6 August 2008 had reported the two candidates virtually tied on the economy, with Obama having about a 2% lead on this subject. That was the situation after seven years of disastrous Bush economic management, with mostly Republican control of Congress — and with Obama having voted with Democrats on the economy more than 90% of the time, and McCain having voted with Republicans on the economy more than 90% of the time. Under these circumstances, Americans should have favored Democratic candidates on the economy by about 95% to 5%. The discrepancy here, of poll-results versus reality, was stunning.

   Also, the October 2008 *CFO* polled nearly 400 big-corporate Chief Financial Officers, and found that 63% preferred McCain, while only 26% favored Obama.

Faith reigned in America, and not just in Pennsylvania.

In 2010, Mike Kimel and Michael E. Kanell came forth with *PRESIMETRICS: What the Facts Tell Us About How the Presidents Measure Up*. This was the first book that examined in detail the economic performance of Presidents. It covered only from Eisenhower through George W. Bush, but some of its data series extended much farther back, as far as 1901. These data spoke volumes, and those volumes were remarkably consistent: Republican Presidents destroyed the economy; Democratic Presidents benefited the economy. Subsequently, Mike Kimel did a number of blog entries under the heading "The Effects of Individual Income Tax Rates on the Economy." These entries decimated Republican trickle-down claims, and documented that wealth percolates up, not trickles down – an economy is more productive if the rich pay far higher tax-rates than everybody else; the extent of economic inequality that exists in America is way beyond having any economic justification at all, and economic history argues for progressive taxation and against conservatives.

Here are some of the findings and conclusions that Kimel stated in his blog entries (and when he referred to "tax rates," he was generally referring to the top marginal tax-rate, the rate that only the richest paid): "Tax rates fell from 77% in 1920 and 1921 to 24% in 1929, the year the Great Depression began. ... In 1932, tax rates rose to 63%, and by 1933, the economy was growing quickly. ... In all but two years from 1933 to 1940, the ... growth rate was faster than in every single year of the Reagan administration. In fact, the average of the yearly growth rates during this period was about a percent and a half faster than Reagan's best year. ... Both the 1901-1928 period and the 1929-1940 period failed to show the [economics] textbook relationship between taxes and growth. In fact, it seems that for both those periods, there was at least a bit of support for the notion that growth was faster in periods of rising tax rates than in periods when tax rates were coming down. There were also a few other findings that might be surprising [to conservatives] – the so-called Roaring 20s were a period in which the economy was often in recession. The New Deal era, on the other hand, coincided with some of the fastest economic growth rates this country has seen since reliable data has been kept. ... In fact, [though] many folks go so far as to say the economy suffered very slow growth until the outbreak of WW2, ... [the data are unequivocal that this] is a comical claim. ... Growth was already fairly quick from 1938 to 1939, and from 1939 to 1940, ... and then it really jumped from 1940 to 1941, [before] the American entry into the war. ... Growth peaked between 1941 and 1942 and then began to shrink."

Referring to more recent times: "The average of the annual growth rates of the 1961 to ... 1964 years when tax rates were 91% was 5.41%. The average from 1966 ... to 1969, after the tax rates were dropped, was 3.49%. ... During seven of the 12 Reagan-Bush years, growth rates were actually below the average rate observed when top marginal tax rates were above 90%. ... Every single year of the Reagan-Bush [era] had a lower average growth rate than when tax rates were in the 60% to 69.9% range. ... Once again, the data fails to show anything resembling the old [the longstanding economists'] 'lower taxes = faster growth' story. In fact, once again, it kind of looks like things go the other way."

A simple explanation of the data would be Marriner S. Eccles's view, that when wealth is highly concentrated, not enough wealth is held by the general public for them to be able to buy much of the services and goods that the economy is offering to them. The rich might buy lots of yachts, but, since their income derives from inheritances, capital gains, dividends, and interest, rather than from wages, much of their income isn't even *spent* on consumption at all – it goes instead into more investments, more gambling. Another, and even simpler, explanation, however, would be that when taxation-rates for the highest-income people are high, those people actually have to work a bit in order to add still further to their mountain of wealth. According to this latter explanation, the nation's economy benefits when aristocrats contribute to it, instead of only or predominantly take from it. When tax-rates are high on the rich, the rich work harder and thus contribute their labor, plus they are paying far more for the roads and bridges and public-school education and police and firemen that benefit *all* businesses – including (but not limited to) businesses that are controlled by aristocrats.

However, progressive economics, of any kind, is not backed by the aristocracy, because most aristocrats – the conservative ones – prefer being leaches on the general welfare, and therefore hire and promote only economists who are their whores. Those economists are the people who write and propagandize "the old [the longstanding economists'] 'lower taxes = faster growth' story," which is false.

The only basis for conservatism is faith. That's why the aristocracy promotes faith. Otherwise, the consequence for aristocrats might *again* be: Off with their heads!

Conservatism Is Based Only on Faith

Max Weber, at the start of the Twentieth Century, published his *The Protestant Ethic and the Spirit of Capitalism*, which asserted that economic prosperity resulted from "the Protestant ethic" which was based upon Luther's concept of "a calling." This faith-based garbage was labeled social "science," and it became too obviously faith-based after Catholic countries such as Ireland started to boom. No one was attributing such booms to "callings," or anything else "Protestant." Then, scholars, like Jared Diamond in his 1997 *Guns Germs and Steel*, said that economic prosperity resulted from fortuitous geography and biology. Historical possibilities such as a President's decisions shaping history were minimized to nothing, though a few more-realistic works had already proven that this view, by Diamond and others, was false. Then, yet more proponents of faith came along, in such works as Rodney Stark's 2005 *The Victory of Reason*, which asserted that the Catholic Church caused prosperity by its theology, which, supposedly, was the very font of "reason."

But that nonsense is equally false, even absurdly so (as if the world needs religious *myths* in order to produce wealth).

What actually causes widespread prosperity is the separation of the Law from God or from any faith-based Scripture, and placing it solely with the individuals who are being ruled by it, that is to say democracy. Economics, in other words, is based upon politics. Capitalism is based upon democracy. Fascism, such as in transitional societies like Nazi Germany or recent China, can advance a national economy only so far, and no further. Democracy is the basis for *real* capitalism (which is called "socialism" in such nations as Norway and France).

This structure of the social sciences is exactly the opposite of the reigning theoretical framework within the social "sciences," which asserts that, instead of economics being based upon politics, politics is based upon economics. Liberals such as Karl Marx (the founder of Communism), and conservatives such as Aaron Director (the founder of the Chicago School), shared that false view, which asserted the supposed fundamentality of economics. If science is to reign in the social fields, that theoretical perspective must be replaced with the scientific view, which is presented here: the progressive, or scientific, understanding of the development of national cultures (including of economics).

No science (in the sense of a field of study which is based upon the epistemology science), social or otherwise, can be based upon false assumptions (such as that economics is fundamental to the law, rather than *vice versa*). False assumptions can be taken only on faith. And, in the social "sciences," they have been.

The fraudulence of economic "science" was noted in *Financial Week*, on 17 December 2008, a year after the Second Great Depression started. Neil Roland headlined there, "Lagging Indicators? Public Beat Economists In Calling the Recession: Majority of Professionals Got the Timing of the Economic Downturn Dead Wrong; Why Is This?" He opened: "Which of two groups — economists or the general public —

came closer to predicting the recession? Surprisingly, it looks like the Joe Six Packs of the world were better economic prognosticators than the elbow patch set." Polls in November 2007, a month before the "recession" started, had shown that whereas 54% of Americans were expecting a recession, only 38% of professional economists were. In a *real* science, the professionals have better predictive ability than do amateurs: All mainstream economists were thus frauds, because no science yet existed in their field — they were all quacks. Even the ones who received Nobels in their field were, because economic *science* hadn't yet started. Economists held opinions — scholars in all fields do. But no scientific basis for those opinions was, as yet, established within the economic profession. It was like physics before Galileo, or biology before Darwin: *pre*-scientific.

Drake Bennett headlined in the Boston *Globe* on 21 December 2008, "Paradigm Lost: Economists Missed the Brewing Crisis," and he reported that there was a widespread recognition by professional economists that their understanding of how an economy functions (and dysfunctions) obviously must be containing important falsehoods, but none of these economists had a clue as to what in their beliefs was false. Even the behavioral economist Richard Thaler, who (along with Daniel Kahneman) had made his reputation mainly by repeatedly experimentally disproving the "rational man" hypothesis (upon which economic theory was based), didn't have a clue. The rules, according to which, people behaved, were not rational (they were faith-based), but even the economists who specialized in economic irrationality didn't truthfully understand their subject, and yet the economists' charade continued as if it hadn't been exposed in the view of anyone who had a scientific outlook. Scholars got away with all they could, and they could get away with anything in an authoritarian culture.

On 26 March 2008, *The New York Times* bannered "A Political Comeback: Supply-Side Economics," and Louis Uchitelle reported that supply-side economics "has become a central tenet of Republican political and economic thinking. That's despite the fact that the big supply-side tax cuts of the 1980s and the 200s did not work out as advertised, as even most supporters acknowledge." The repeated failures of this theory, to predict accurately (which is the test of *any* theory in science), had done virtually nothing to kill this theory off in economic "science"; and so Republicans were still able to promote their supply-side proposals and not be hooted out of the economics profession — a profession of quacks, professional whores of their "expertise" (or propaganda) to and for the aristocracy, fooling the public to shove yet-more unearned wealth to the already-wealthy. Of course, there were also a few economists who derided supply-side economics: "'The supply-side argument these days really applies to upper-income people,' said Robert M. Solow, a Nobel laureate in economics who served in the Kennedy administration. 'They are portrayed as the golden geese, and you don't want to discourage them from laying their [golden] eggs.'" But Republican economists weren't being *excluded from the profession*, as would have happened if economics were a scientific field — there was nothing at all like the exclusion of creationists from the biological professions. In fact, believers in the "invisible hand" of God *were* the economics profession; and the most-prized economic whores were typically the ones who received the best-endowed teaching chairs; the aristocrats paid their propagandists handsomely.

The economics profession was so bad that, after Bush's White House years became just past history, and the nation was already collapsing into another Great Depression, which should have proven, to anyone with a scientific outlook the failure of economic theory, economists *continued* believing their garbage. One of the rare exceptions was economist James Galbraith, who headlined in the March 2009 *Washington Monthly*, "Why the Economic Crisis, and Its Solution, Are Bigger than You Think," and he wrote: "The deepest belief of the modern economist is that the economy is a self-stabilizing system. This means that, even if nothing is done, normal rates of employment and production will someday return. Practically all modern economists believe this, often without thinking much about it." He there defined the "invisible hand." The economics profession had still learned nothing from history; they remained scholars. In fact, the new Democratic President loaded his Administration with economists such as the failed Lawrence Summers, who during his time in Bill Clinton's Administration had joined Robert Rubin in leading the charge to prevent the regulation of derivatives. Summers also led the charge for the Republicans' Gramm-Leach-Bliley Act which ended FDR's separation of investment banks from commercial banks and so helped bring on the 2008 crash. Even Democrats believed in the myth of the "invisible hand" of God. They simply weren't as fanatical about it as Republicans were. Whereas Republicans were fundamentalist Christians, Democrats were liberal Christians — but still, they based their beliefs largely upon faith. That's why the new Democratic President, Barack Obama, hired for his Administration Summers and other failed Clinton economists. Obama wasn't as bad as Bush, nor as bad as McCain would have been, but he was still bad.

On 23 July 2008, Reuters headlined "Majority of Economists See McCain Better for Stocks," and reported that, "On a scale of 1 to 5, with 5 being 'very good,' 12 economists gave [the Republican U.S. Presidential candidate, John] McCain's proposals higher marks, ... and eight preferred [the Democratic candidate, Barack] Obama's policies." This survey didn't sample opinions from astrologers, but would have been at least as reliable a predictive indicator on the economy, from a scientific standpoint, if it had done so. Evidence indicated overwhelmingly that Obama would be far better for the U.S. economy than would McCain, but economists discounted such evidence, when they didn't outright ignore it altogether. But no matter: Like with the Delphic priests, their opinions held authority, within their overwhelmingly religious culture and society. (However, a Democratic economist, Brad DeLong, was more honest, when he blogged on 5 January

2011, "What Have We Learned From The Great Recession?" and concluded that: "Macroeconomics should be banned," and that "Macroeconomics should be taught only through economic history and the history of economic thought," like the garbage which constitute academic philosophy is. He was saying that to call economics yet a "science," as the Nobel Committee did, was clearly a gross misunderstanding, if not an outright lie.)

After Obama was elected on 4 November 2008 to follow the Presidency of George W. Bush, the previously optimistic view of the U.S. economy which had been exhibited by Republicans in all pre-election polls turned sharply negative, despite the overwhelmingly documented fact that not just the economy but also the stock and bond markets do far better under Democratic presidents, and under Democratic congresses, than under Republican ones – and Democrats now controlled *all three*. Republican voters are utterly immune to facts that don't comport with the lies they've committed themselves to. It's how conservative politicians win political office even in democracies. On 10 December 2008, CNBC bannered "Americans See Brighter Economic Future: Survey," and reported: "Democrats are twice as optimistic about the economy as they were in September; Republicans are nearly twice as pessimistic." Moreover, "The answer [to the optimism question] breaks sharply along party lines, with 78 percent of Democrats and 24 percent of Republicans believing Obama's election will improve the economy. Independents were split down the middle." Republicans, like so many economists, held faith in trickle-down from God's People. Worshipping The Almighty, they believed that God's People should continue to rule — that it was the will of God, and that the will of God was right and the will of Man was sinful and wrong. They believed that the change from George W. Bush to Barack Obama would constitute a threat, rather than a relief, to the U.S. economy.

But science and democracy indicate to the contrary: Letting power have free reign over economics is not constructive for the public's welfare — God's Law is not as good for the public as is democracy. And Paul's positive achievement was to separate the Law from God, and so to permit democracy to develop within his new religious culture. The same man who created the world's largest religion has also laid the foundation for science to take over politics, and thus to weaken religion, and perhaps ultimately end the Religious Age.

Two days after Democrat Barack Obama swept the 4 November 2008 U.S. Presidential election, the *Wall Street Journal* bannered "New Debt Could Hamstring Obama: Sharp Rise in Treasury Borrowing Seen Pressuring New Programs, Tax-Cut Agenda." Jon Hilsenrath reported that, "Economists project that total government borrowing could pass $1.5 trillion in the fiscal year, which ends next September, pushing up the government's total debt burden by more than 25% in one year." An accompanying chart was titled "Bigger Burden: U.S. Public Debt." It showed that until Republican President Ronald Reagan entered office in 1981, the U.S. public debt as a percentage of GDP was stable; it then immediately skyrocketed starting in 1982, and it plateaued almost as soon as Democratic President Bill Clinton entered the White House in 1993. It actually declined during the period from 1997-2000. This percentage then soared again during each year of George W. Bush's Presidency.

Some Republican scholars try to blame the first Great Depression on Democratic President Franklin Delano Roosevelt, who was actually swept into the Oval Office in 1933 precisely because the Great Depression was already well under way, from his Republican predecessor, following more than a decade of Republican mismanagement of the U.S. economy. Voteview.ucsd.edu posted a graph, "Real Per Capita Income: 1920 – 1970 (1958 Prices)," which showed PCI bottoming in 1933, and soaring immediately thereafter, almost uninterrupted, until 1945, when war-debts had to be paid down. One of the reasons PCI soared after FDR came into office is that the unemployment rate when he entered office was 24.9%, and it gradually declined to 14.3% in 1937, and briefly rose again to 19% in 1938 (after a brief interruption in FDR's Keynesian priming of the economic pump), and then promptly declined again, down to 10% in 1941, and then even lower as WWII got under way. The economic performance of Democrat FDR was as superb as the economic performance of his Republican predecessors had been disastrous.

Democrats were coming into office in 2009 in order to, yet again, get the U.S. economy moving, after lengthy Republican misrule had led it to a near-death experience. Clearly, when a government chosen by the Moral Majority, and other theocratic Christians, took over the U.S. Government in 1981, they commenced a process which ultimately destroyed the U.S. economy. And, now, President Barack Obama and his Democratic Congress would need to pick up the pieces, following the mess which conservatives had, yet again, created.

But even Democrats were, to a large extent, flying blind, at least as regards the insights required for this enormous task from professional economists. On 21 December 2008, the *Chicago Tribune's* Frank James headlined at swamppolitics.com, "Paul Krugman's Horror Story," and he quoted from a recent speech by that year's economics Nobelist, and NYT columnist, Paul Krugman, in which Dr. Krugman acknowledged that economists still — in 2008 — didn't yet know what had caused the first Great Depression to end. Krugman said that WWII, "a large public works program," "ended" it, but not *really*, because:

"What we really still don't understand very well is why, when the war was over, the Depression didn't come back. We actually don't know that very well. And that's a question that I think we're going to want to think about quite a lot, in its modern guise, as we look forward. Scary times."

Flying blind into an economic hurricane is, indeed, "scary," at least as scary as flying blind in physics was before Galileo and Newton, and as flying blind in biology was before Darwin

and Mendel. (What must it have been like, for example, to
undergo a medical operation in such a time?) FDR's first bout
of "public works programs" had ameliorated the Great
Depression, but didn't end it. Why did WWII end it? No one
actually knew; and in fact, no one really knew whether WWII
did end it. Economic theory wasn't yet scientific, and thus
economic practice remained still scholarly, not scientific, and
so there remained plenty of room for professional economists
to disagree among themselves about such important economic
policy-issues — and there was little real guidance they could
provide, even in areas where they did largely agree.

So, history was being repeated, and this was history
from which economists (being scholars instead of scientists)
had unfortunately learned little or nothing.

The first Great Depression, the one during the 1930's,
actually came after Republicans had reigned within both
houses of Congress since 1918, and had reigned the White
House since 1920; Republicans had ruled all three places for a
very long time; and then in 1932, Democrats suddenly swept
all three, and ruled without challenge until Republicans again
took both houses of Congress in 1946. The Presidency
remained Democratic straight from 1932 through to 1952. A
faithful America swept Republicans back into power in all
three places during the 1952 elections, and thus started the
nation back onto the kleptocratic road, which became clearer
in 1980, and clearer still in 2000, leading to the crash in 2008,
ending a lengthy Republican hegemony as had happened in
the 1920's.

Near the end of Bush's White House years, Eric
Lichtblau headlined in *The New York Times*, on Tuesday, 9
September 2008, "Antitrust Document Exposes Rift." Bush's
Administration had just bailed out Fannie Mae and Freddie
Mac two days earlier, which was only his second bailout after
his having bailed out JPMorgan Chase's acquisition of the
collapsing Bear Stearns company months earlier, on March
16th. Bush was now bailing out his former top financial
backers, one after another. But this evidently wasn't enough to

satisfy him. Lichtblau reported "a rift between the Justice Department and the Federal Trade Commission over whether the government was protecting consumers or big businesses. ... Three of the four commissioners on the F.T.C. issued a statement saying that the policy" of the "Justice" Department "was 'a blueprint for radically weakened enforcement' against anticompetitive practices. They said the Justice Department guidelines allowed monopolies to act 'with impunity' and 'would make it nearly impossible to prosecute a case.' In nearly eight years under the Bush administration, the Justice Department has brought one case against a business on anticompetitive grounds," and it was only a minor case, concerning a West Virginia newspaper. But even Bush's own FTC was now alarmed about this new initiative of his "Justice" Department, to make monopolies virtually scot-free of any effective regulations at all. The reason these three FTC commissioners were concerned is that the 2006 mid-term congressional elections had so weakened Bush, that his control of the FTC now faltered: The four-member Commission's three rebels consisted of one independent, one Democrat, and one Republican, and the only remaining Bush loyalist on the FTC was its second Republican (whom Bush had made the Commission's Chairman only a few months earlier). By contrast, Bush still controlled the "Justice" Department *100%*.

Trickle-Down vs. Percolate-Up Economics

The doctrine of the beneficence of the "invisible hand" of God was introduced by Adam Smith in his 1776 *Wealth of Nations*, in order to hide the theocratic underpinning of the aristocracy's preferred ideology. There was no science of economics whatsoever. This was merely a way to rationalize the wealth of the already-wealthy.

Of course, Milton Friedman, the late Nobel-winning economist, and king of conservative economics, agreed with the rest of "the Chicago School," and with its "Law and

Economics Movement," in opposing antitrust, and in supporting monopoly, oligopoly, cartels, and corporate bigness in general. All of these University of Chicago economic movements were founded by so-called "libertarians," who favored liberty for the aristocrats, and who were opposed to any government to the extent the government served the demos, the public (or was "democratic"). Nazi leaders had the same attitude towards government: it's good only if it's dictatorial and imposes God's Law and not the Law or constitution of any authentic *public*. Fascism is *only* for God's People.

On 5 January 2009, the liberal Keynesian economist Paul Krugman's *N.Y. Times* column was titled "Fighting Off Depression"; and now, at the very end of Bush's term of office destroying America if not the world, Krugman said, "This looks an awful lot like the beginning of a second Great Depression"; and Krugman largely blamed the depression-theorist Friedman for this economic disaster, by saying: "Friedman's claim that monetary policy could have prevented the Great Depression was an attempt to refute the analysis of John Maynard Keynes, who argued that monetary policy is ineffective under depression conditions and that fiscal policy — large-scale deficit spending by the government — is needed to fight mass unemployment. The failure of monetary policy in the current crisis shows that Keynes had it right." However, George W. Bush had always been running huge fiscal deficits; and the real problem wasn't how much his government was spending, but rather what that spending was buying, and who was paying the taxes to fund it. A better reading of the economic situation would thus have been: kleptocracy steals from the public, and that's very bad. Economic theory ignores distributional issues (on account of Pareto optimality); and, therefore, even the very *idea* of "kleptocracy" has no relevance to it.* Conservatives defend kleptocrats — that's what

---

* The only aspect of theft that's opposed by Pareto optimality is a (presumably forced) transfer of property which leaves the victim poorer. In reality,

economists have no business evaluating transfers of property, and they ignore distributions of property — which *is* their business. Pareto optimality prohibits consideration of *any existing distribution of wealth*, even if that existing distribution is one in which a single person owns all the wealth, and in which all others are his slaves. In economic theory, that king-slaves economy is equally "efficient" or "optimal" as is one in which wealth is equally distributed.

Obviously, this theory was designed by fascists. Pareto was himself praised by Mussolini and sometimes called "the Karl Marx of fascism." It's easy to understand why. Calling a field "scientific" which is based upon principles that can be accepted only on faith, is to lie, as economists routinely do.

In 2007, a volume edited by Edward Fullbrook, *Real World Economics*, documented the increasing disrepute of the economics profession for its fraudulence, and the economist Herbert Gintis panned it at amazon.com, because he saw that volume as nothing but an affirmation of laziness from economics students who didn't want to put in the enormous effort that's required in order to learn the intricate mathematics of the field. This was the same Herbert Gintis who had co-authored with Samuel Bowles and Melissa Groves the 2005 *Unequal Chances: Family Background and Economic Success [in America]*. That book documented and bemoaned America's recently (since the Ronald Reagan Administration) becoming a fairly rigid class-based society. Behind that documentation stood much of the intricate mathematics which Gintis was now implicitly equating with economics. However, absent from the bemoaning was anything in economic theory itself which could possibly warrant any such bemoaning of this change in the U.S. economy. Gintis, like most economists, never noticed this failure of economic theory, but this failure was largely to blame for the justifiable rapidly declining respect in which the economics profession was held. Contempt for the economics profession didn't have to be associated with laziness of any kind; it was, instead, primarily, a call for a "Real World Economic" theory, which might entail the same mathematics as the old mental gyrations that supported the theory behind the "invisible hand" of God. Perhaps some students did rebel against learning complex math in order to become able to understand a false economic theory, but the problem there lies not with the "lazy" students; the problem lies with the false theory. The fact that even an economist, who bemoans America's becoming a class-based society, is insensitive to his profession's irrelevance to that change, is a better demonstration of the failure of the economics profession than is anything that's presented in *Real World Economics*. It shows how deep-seated the failure of the economics profession actually is.

One doesn't have to be an economist in order to be able to document changes in the economy; it requires some math but no economic theory. Economic theory is needed in order to be able to evaluate changes in the economy; and when an economist bemoans the concentration of more and more wealth in fewer and fewer hands, or the intergenerational rigidity of economic classes, there's nothing in current economic theory to *justify* that negative evaluation. The math in economics isn't the problem; the falseness of economic theory is the problem. Economists will remain the embodiment of the problem until they come to recognize the falseness of their theory. If they don't recognize that it's false, they won't replace it with a theory that's true. The only thing that makes those people economists is the theory

conservatism is all about: "justifying" white-collar criminality
and the entire trickle-down system. That's the problem with
the economics of Milton Friedman, George W. Bush, and all
other extreme conservatives.

The prior day's *NYT*, on January 4th, had featured a
lengthy article by Joe Nocera in the Sunday magazine, "Risk
Mismanagement," which presented the financial melt-down
as having resulted from a technical error in financial firms'
calculation of "Value at Risk," and not from a sick culture, and
an unscientific economic profession which did all it could to
ignore white-collar crime and to focus obsessively upon lower
class crimes. Eight days afterward, Bernard Wasow at The
Century Foundation headlined "Act of God? No, House of
Cards," and he appropriately rejected that analysis of the
problem: "The key question academics and policy makers
should be asking is how it was possible for the people who
trade in long-term contracts to derive their rewards on the
basis of short-term results," Wasow said. "With employees of
financial institutions drawing fat rewards as if they were day
laborers paid by the number of financial bricks they could lay,
hardly anyone bothered if the edifice they were constructing

---

they've mastered, but this theory is false and needs to be replaced. Until it's
replaced with a theory that's true, economists will deserve the public's contempt.

Already in 2001, Steve Keen's classic *Debunking Economics: The Naked
Emperor of the Social Sciences* was published in Australia, exposing a number of
demonstrated falsehoods among the axioms or assumptions of economics. The
question now for economists was the same one that pre-scientific, Earth-centric,
physics, or "natural philosophy," faced during the decades and centuries before
Galileo came along and created the *science* of physics: How can we replace a
mathematical system that's based upon false axioms? And the answer is also the
same: *Replace the false axioms with true ones.*

Also, the reason for the false axioms was the same: The purpose of those
axioms was to sustain the prevailing religion, the Bible. Instead of sustaining the
Creation story, as natural philosophy did, economic faith sustained the "invisible
hand" of God, the belief that the distribution of wealth was right because it's what
God wanted, and that therefore anyone or anything which would reallocate wealth
(such as progressive taxation) is "inefficient" or bad. This is how we came to
develop a system of economic "science" that couldn't even recognize the evilness
of slavery: It was actually economic *faith.*

was functional or safe. This was construction without structural engineers and without working building codes. Preventing future financial/economic crises has almost nothing to do with better financial modeling. It has everything to do with aligning rewards with the work done." The entire top-down culture was looking the other way, not looking at the actual source of the problem — which was at the top.

On the last day of Bush's Presidency, NYU economist Nouriel Roubini, speaking in Dubai, calculated the first draft for a comprehensive accounting of the immediate economic wreckage Bush's Presidency had produced. Bloomberg News headlined on 20 January 2009, "Roubini Predicts U.S. Losses May Reach $3.6 Trillion," and reported that, "U.S. financial losses from the credit crisis may reach $3.6 trillion, suggesting the banking system is 'effectively insolvent,' said New York University Professor Nouriel Roubini, who predicted last year's economic crisis. 'I've found that credit losses could peak at a level of $3.6 trillion for U.S. institutions, half of them by banks and broker dealers. ... If that's true, it means the U.S. banking system is effectively insolvent because it starts with a capital of $1.4 trillion.'" Roubini, who had been one of only a handful of economists who had predicted the credit-collapse and depression, recommended FDR-era letter-agencies — the HOLC, RFC, and RTC — as the most effective policy-responses.

Economic theory offered little real guidance (and Milton Friedman's monetarism was by now outright disproven), but economic history was clear: progressive politics produces rising economies, and conservative politics produces sinking ones. Faith says otherwise, but faith is always associated with false beliefs, and no belief in the field of economics is as firmly established scientifically, as that democracy produces economic success for a country, and that aristocracy and theocracy produce economic failure.

One of Friedman's fellow extremist conservatives in the Economics Department at the University of Chicago was fellow-Nobelist Gary Becker, who on 21 March 2009 was the subject of an interview on the op-ed page of the *Wall Street Journal*. Headlining there "Now Is No Time to Give Up on Markets," he kept the aristocratic fascist faith in the "invisible hand" of God, and opposed its becoming subordinated to the visible hand of Man via democracy. He was unapologetic about any of his numerous false predictions, and about his long record of having favored conservative candidates over ones who preferred democratic government. He continued to support the policies that he had always supported, and he condemned the policies of the new Democratic President, Barack Obama. "Mr. Becker sees the finger prints [sic] of big government all over today's economic woes." Becker didn't condemn Republican economic policies that had gotten the nation into this mess, but instead such things as "the Community Reinvestment Act in the '70s and then Fannie Mae and Freddie Mac later on," which "put many unqualified borrowers into the mix." The policies that Becker and the Republicans during the prior eight years had imposed upon the economy were held blameless. If a criminal's first act which indicates the possibility of having become reformed is an acknowledgement of guilt and an expression of deep shame for his crimes, then Gary Becker should have been locked up for life, but so should all Republicans, if there had been space enough in U.S. prisons to hold them. They had done far more damage to the United States of America than had the people who currently were in prison. Becker held the faith, just as did Milton Friedman, that the best fiscal policy is no fiscal policy, and that government expenditures in a democracy are *intrinsically* wasteful. "Keynesianism was out of fashion for so long that ... there is almost no evidence on what the multiplier would be. ... I think it would be well below one." The basic fascist view of economics didn't change, and it was that the *only* valid expenditures by government are for military and police — if even *that*. (Aristocrats behind the gated walls of their compounds tend to prefer relying upon their own, *privately* paid, police forces, and upon direct payoffs to government officials, since these aristocrats' money then doesn't go to protect anyone but themselves.)

The 30 March 2009 *Newsweek* featured as its cover story "The Outrage Factor," concerning the public's response to Wall Street's psychopathy, and included an essay from Wall Street's most-effective policeman, former N.Y. Attorney General, Eliot Spitzer, "Making Up for Years of Neglect." He explained why the Law-and-Economics movement, and also so-called libertarianism itself, were false; and he described how, in contrast to such mythologizers, laws precede, and do not follow, any capitalist economy. He explained the falseness of the theoretical foundations of American fascism.

In July 2011, the Levy Economics Institute issued one of the most important papers in all of economics, "What Ended the Great Depression? Reevaluating the Role of Fiscal Policy" by Nathan Perry and Matias Vernengo. They found that historical data debunked Milton Friedman's theory that monetary policy (the Fed) had caused the Great Depression and that Fed policy-reversal alone had ended it. This Perry/Vernengo paper proved that the President's economic policies, called "fiscal policy," were the chief determinants of economic activity; the Fed's monetary policies were not. "Conventional wisdom [among the economics profession] contends that fiscal policy was of secondary importance to the economic recovery in the 1930s." Filling out that viewpoint, but unfortunately ignored by these authors, was Robert A. Margo's "Employment and Unemployment in the 1930s," in the Spring 1993 *Journal of Economic Perspectives*. Margo had explained that the statistics economists cite for unemployment during the Great Depression count as being "Unemployed" the millions of people who were actually employed by the Government, in Works Progress Administration (WPA), etc. In other words, economists were automatically disqualifying these Federal workers from the category "Employed," and were calling them "Unemployed." Economists were assuming that when FDR provided government-paid work to unemployed people, not only was this money being wasted, but the direct beneficiaries weren't even receiving the benefit

of a job. This false assumption grossly overestimated
"Unemployment" under FDR. Restoring those people, whom
the Government had employed building and repairing
bridges, etc., to the "Employed" category, produced the
following annual percentages as being "Unemployed": 1932:
22.9%. 1933: 20.6%. 1934: 16.0%. 1935: 14.2%. 1936: 9.9%. 1937:
9.1%. 1938: 12.5%. 1939: 11.3%. 1940: 9.5%. When I pointed this
out online in response to an article at businessinsider.com
(headlined "Roubini and Soros Say The US Is In A Double Dip
And Warn Of An Uprising"), on 25 September 2011, there was
this reply, from "Anti":
    "Even using Robert A. Margo's questionable numbers
for those years [and 'Anti' didn't say what was 'questionable'
about that], Hitler was the hands down winner as far as
managing a nation's economy – and with a minimum of
military spending. The US 1939 number was improved over
1938 because of US military spending for the war which FDR
wanted and did so much to bring about. America, if it had a
brain, could learn so much from Hitler – like striving for
energy independence as Hitler did with only coal as a
resource. From coal, Nazi Germany sought to make
everything from gasoline to chemicals and pharmaceuticals –
and to a great extent, they succeeded – and even fought a
world war against overwhelming odds for six years. T. Boone
Pickens who has some extremely sane proposals for utilizing
US natural gas for long haul trucking for example, can hardly
get anyone to listen to him – least of all in Washington."
    "Anti" self-identified by linking to a Holocaust-denial
website: nazigassings.com, which proudly claimed to be a
"website that denies the Holocaust hoax."
    Fascism is just as much of a hoax as is Christianity (or
any other religion) itself, and just as enduring.
    And even liberals ignore the extent to which
progressivism is confirmed by history. For example, Henry
Blodget, the founder of businessinsider.com and formerly the
flunky who had taken the fall for Merrill Lynch's Republican

CEO Stanley O'Neal and who paid multimillion-dollar fines for one of Merrill's frauds (for his doing O'Neal's bidding), headlined on 17 December 2011, "Well, It Sure Seems Like Keynes Was Right," and he said, "What was World War 2 if not an absolutely gigantic Keynesian stimulus?" Regardless of whether WWII was a "stimulus," war isn't necessary in order for a nation to recover from decades of conservative government. But one thing that *is* necessary in order to recover from conservatism is progressivism.

Republicans Harm More than *Just* the Economy

On 2 August 2011, the major book by James Gilligan was published: *Why Some Politicians Are More Dangerous to Your Health than Others*. He documents there such things as, "According to the most objective and reliable data that we have concerning prosperity and public safety, the Republican party is the party of poverty and violent death." He claims that throughout the entire period 1900-2007, all Republican presidencies experienced increasing rates of not just unemployment, but also of poverty, suicides, and homicides, whereas all Democratic presidencies saw decreasing rates of each of those four. His data are actually slightly less stunning than he claims, because his graph, Figure B1, on page 206, shows that "Violent deaths per 100,000 population per year" actually *rose* during 1960-68, while Democrats were in the White House. However, the data on the two pages following that do show that, *without exception*, throughout the period tabulated there, extending from 1948-2003, unemployment rates went down during each Democratic Presidency, and the average length of a person's unemployment got shorter during each Democratic Presidency; and that the exact opposite happened whenever a Republican was occupying the White House. The probability that such stunning outcomes occurred randomly is virtually nil. Certainly, as a general rule, if not as an iron rule, *only* people who are evil and/or misinformed vote Republican. You cannot know the historical record and vote Republican (unless a person is anti-American, that is).

Republican propaganda to the contrary is just the fascist Big Lie, in America. No tolerably well-informed person (other than a traitorous and super-greedy aristocrat) would vote Republican, and virtually only majoritarian religious individuals *do* vote Republican (just as had happened in 1930's Germany, 1980 Iran, and other countries that democratically *chose* their fascist party to lead).

Would Romney Be Better than Obama?

The Presidential choice in 2012 is, of course, between Barack Obama and Mitt Romney. However, based upon all of this evidence, *any* Democrat will almost certainly be considerably better than *any* Republican, or at least considerably less bad than the Republican would be. When the historical differences between the performance-records of the two Parties are this extreme, the *individual* differences between the candidates who are opposing each other in any given election are far less important than those two candidates' *Party-affiliations*.

For whatever reason, the ideological differences between these two Parties are that stark, and Democratic policy-ideas have been proven by history to be that much truer than are Republican policy-ideas, so that the simple rule-of-thumb, **any Democrat is better than any Republican**, will provide more-reliable guidance for a voter than will any estimation of the two opponents that's based upon more complicated considerations, which would be merely gratuitous because less reliable (given the enormous disparity in performance-records of these two Parties).

That's how *extreme* the differences are, between the *actual historical records* of these two political Parties.

In other words, however bad a President Obama might be or is, Romney would probably be worse.

However, on 21 May 2012, Gallup headlined "Obama, Romney Each Has Economic Strengths With Americans," and reported that when Americans were asked "if you think Barack Obama or Mitt Romney would better handle each of the following issues," Romney had a 15% advantage over Obama on "The federal budget deficit and debt," a 10% advantage on "Economic growth," and a 14% advantage on "The financial performance of Americans' savings and retirement accounts." These expectations directly contradicted the overwhelming historical evidence that was based upon the two Parties' actual historical records, which was unequivocally in the opposite direction. If Romney's economic recommendations had been strikingly outside of the Republican norm, then there would have been a scientifically based reason for Americans to consider – not necessarily to hold, but just to *consider* holding – these beliefs, but that was not at all the case here. In fact, Romney had endorsed the House Republican budget drawn up by the far-right Congressman Paul Ryan (the head of the House Budget Committee), and he also endorsed Ryan's new budget plan, "The Path to Prosperity," though the centrist Tax Policy Center calculated that its reduction in the top tax-rate would increase the federal debt by $1 trillion over ten years, its corporate tax-reduction would increase that by another $900 billion, and its elimination of the Alternative Minimum Tax (without replacement) would increase that debt by yet another $650 billion. The Congressional Budget Office calculated that the plan's elimination of Obamacare would further increase that debt by yet another $800 billion, and IRS data indicated that its elimination of the 15% tax-bracket would add at least another $1 trillion on top of that. Furthermore, the historical record provided no support whatsoever to the public's expectation that these tax-cuts to the rich and to corporations would boost American stock markets. It was all fantasy. The historical record from previous polls showed that this was normal fantasy: the *same* counterfactual public expectations had been expressed during virtually all previous elections.

References/Sources

The Hyacinth Editions "house style" is designed to facilitate any reader's access to the sources. Therefore, this work cites predominantly sources that are widely available on the internet, because most readers have ready access to the internet. The aim here is to cite not just credible sources, but credible sources that are available on the web, and that the individual reader can thus readily access without needing to visit a first-rate library (which might be some distance away, or otherwise inaccessible).

The manner of citation of internet-accessible sources here is via a quotation (which may be a headline, or the title of a given work), and its date (either byline- or publication-date), and the name of the news-medium or other publisher from which the report first appeared, and the author. One or more of those four items, if employed in a web-search, will normally bring up the cited source. This makes as easy as possible the reader's exploration of the sources.

In some instances (especially when a given source is no longer directly available on the web), the URL for a source is given, which may be found (if not directly in a web-search) by means of the Wayback Machine (archive.org).

Since references and sources are provided within the text, there is no need for – no benefit to providing – a separate bibliography, and so none is presented here.

Made in the USA
Lexington, KY
04 July 2012